I CONFESS ONE BAPTISM...

I CONFESS ONE BAPTISM...

Protopresbyter George D. Metallinos, D. Th., Ph. D.
Dean of the University of Athens, School of Theology

Interpretation and application of Canon VII
of the Second Ecumenical Council by the *Kollyvades* and
Constantine Oikonomos

(A contribution to the historico-canonical evaluation of the
problem of the validity of Western baptism)

Uncut Mountain Press

I CONFESS ONE BAPTISM...

© 1994, 2024
Uncut Mountain Press

All rights reserved under International and Pan-American Copyright Conventions.

uncutmountainpress.com

Scriptural quotations are primarily taken from the King James Version. The translator has emended some quotations to better reflect the original Greek text. Citations from the Psalms are primarily taken from The Psalter According to the Seventy, translated from the Septuagint Version of the Old Testament by the Holy Transfiguration Monastery, Brookline, MA.

Library of Congress Cataloging-in-Publication Data
Protopresbyter George D. Metallinos, D. Th., Ph. D., 1940–2019

I Confess One Baptism—2nd English ed.
Translated by Priestmonk Seraphim
Edited by Uncut Mountain Press
Footnotes beginning with "Ed." are added to this second edition by Uncut Mountain Press.

ISBN (softcover): 978-1-63941-071-2
ISBN (digital): 978-1-63941-072-9

The first English edition is a translation and edited version, with additional material of the book in Greek by the same title, Ομολογώ εν Βάπτισμα, which was published by the author in Athens in 1983.

First Printed by St. Paul's Monastery, Holy Mountain, 1994
630 87 DAPHNE, Greece
ISBN 960-85542-0-9

I. Eastern Orthodox Christian Theology
II. Eastern Orthodox Christian Ecclesiology

CANON VII

of the Second Ecumenical Council, Constantinople, 381 A.D.

On how heretics are to be received:

As for heretics who convert to Orthodoxy and join the portion of the saved, we receive them in accordance with the following procedure and custom: We receive Arians, and Macedonians, and Sabbatians, and Novatians who call themselves Catharoi and Aristeroi, and Tessareskaidekatitæ otherwise known as Tetraditæ, and Apollinarists, when they submit written statements, and anathematize every heresy that does not believe as the holy, catholic, and Apostolic Church of God believes, and are first sealed with holy Myron on the forehead, and the eyes, and the nose, and the mouth, and the ears; and in sealing them we say: "Seal of the gift of the Holy Spirit."

Eunomians, on the other hand, who are baptized with one immersion, and Montanists who in this [City] are called Phrygians, and Sabellians who teach the son-fatherhood [of Christ], and who do other evil things as well; and all other heresies (for there are many hereabout, especially those hailing from the region of the Galatians), all of them that wish to join Orthodoxy we receive as pagans. And on the first day we make them Christians; on the second, catechumens. Then on the third day we exorcise them with the threefold blowing into their face and ears. And then we catechize them, and oblige them to spend sufficient time in the church and to listen to the Scriptures. And then we baptize them.

CONTENTS

Foreword 8

Preface to the Greek Edition 11

Preface to the English Edition 13

Abbreviations 17

Introduction 19

I. The Principal Figures 26
    1. The "*Kollyvades*" Fathers of the Holy Mountain 26
    2. Constantine Oikonomos of the Oikonomoi 32
    3. Cyril V, Patriarch of Constantinople 34

II. Interpretation of the Canon 38
    1. Ecclesiological and Canonical Presuppositions 38
    2. Authenticity of the Canon 44
    3. Interpretation of the Canon 52
    4. Summary 66

III. Application of the Canon 68
    1. Latins are "heretics" and "unbaptized" 69
    2. Latins are "in need of baptism" 73
    3. Explanation of the Orthodox Church's Action
    in Dealing with the Latins 82
        a) Until the Council of Florence 85
        b) After Florence 90

IV. Critical Evaluation **98**
1. The Position of the Ecumenical Patriarchate 98
2. The Action of Patriarch Cyril V 102
3. The Policy in Russia 110

Epilogue **113**

Appendix I **120**
Holy Canons Dealing with Baptism
    a) Canons of the Holy Apostles 120
    b) Canons of Ecumenical Councils 121
    c) Local Councils 125
    d) The Canonical Letters of St. Basil the Great 129

Appendix II **135**
Oros of the holy Great Church of Christ
on the Baptism of Converts from the West
(1755/56)

Appendix III **139**
(Re)baptism of Latins on the Ionian Islands
in the Nineteenth Century

Appendix IV **144**
Letter to the Œcumenical Patriarch Saint Gregory V
from Saint Nikodemus the Hagiorite

Appendix V **146**
That Those Returning from the Latins Must
Incontrovertibly, Indispensably, and Necessarily
Be Baptized, by Saint Athanasius of Paros

FOREWORD

Ὅ ἦν ἀπ᾽ ἀρχῆς, ὃ ἀκηκόαμεν,
ὃ ἑωράκαμεν, ἀπαγγέλλομεν ὑμῖν.
(1 Jn. 1:1)

WHAT IS ORTHODOXY? Orthodoxy is correct practice (...*the Way*), correct dogma (...*the Truth*), correct knowledge of God (...*eternal Life*); the Word of God, the Word delivered, the Word transmitted; the Transmitter, the Tradition...Christ Himself.

And who is Orthodox? Orthodox are the holy Fathers and Mothers of our Church. These are the God-bearers, the Saints; Christified, deified; the rule and measure of Orthodoxy, because they have Him dwelling and abiding in themselves.

We who by the unspeakable goodness of Divine Providence have underservingly been counted worthy to inhabit the Holy Mountain Athos—this blessed Garden of our All-holy Lady Theotokos—have been vouchsafed in our turn to receive through our holy Fathers in God the divine Tradition of our Orthodox faith, the sacred deposit, the very Pearl of great price itself.

This Tradition we hold more valuable than all else, being as it is eternal Truth. To be sure, by virtue of its divine nature it is invulnerable and invincible; susceptible to errors are imperfect, unperfected human beings; some to make them, and others to suffer the sometimes enduring effects. Understandably, though, we view with apprehension anything that would purpose to alter or misrepresent the Tradition and undermine its authenticity, as a threat to the welfare of mankind which is saved only by the Truth.

Heeding the divine injunction which commands that he who loves God love his brethren also, we feel obliged to contribute to the preservation of the saving Truth within the human race, in the small measure of our own abilities. Hence, glorifying our all-benevolent God without whom we can accomplish nothing good, we proceed with the publication of the English version of Fr. George D. Metallinos' enlightening study, *I Confess One Baptism*. We do so with sober joy and humble satisfaction, anticipating as we do the benefit to our contemporaries that this book will bring, inasmuch as we believe it is an accurate exposition and expression of our Orthodox Christian Tradition and of the patristic mind and teaching on the particular subject with which it deals.

The original Greek text of *I Confess One Baptism*, published in 1983 and currently out of print, was written in Katharevusa, and many passages quoted therein are in an even older form of the Greek Language. The author worked closely with our translator for meaning. Nevertheless something is inevitably lost in the translation, except perhaps the telltale signs of translation itself, for which (and every other shortcoming) we beg the indulgence of the discriminating reader.

This publication would have remained beyond the potentials of our Monastery had it not been for the cooperation of friends and supporters. We would like to thank Archimandrite Damian of the Monastery of the Glorious Ascension, Frs. Paisios and Benedict of Philotheou

Monastery, Reader Vladimir Phelan, Mr. Demetrios Christaphacopoulos, and Miss Elizabeth Papps for their invaluable encouragement and assistance. The entire responsibility, however, for the form and content of this book lies exclusively with St. Paul's Monastery.

✠ Archimandrite Parthenios
St. Paul's Monastery on the Holy Mountain
Sunday of the Holy Fathers of the Holy Mountain, 1994

PREFACE TO THE GREEK EDITION

IN THE theological dialogues of our time, the holy sacraments are the center of discussion. Much has been said in the precincts of the Ecumenical Movement about unity and agreement in the sacraments. It follows that this should be even more so the case with holy baptism, the sacrament by which entrance into the Church is accomplished. It is therefore absolutely necessary that the full extent of the patristic tradition's position be sufficiently known in these discussions, so that the course of navigation towards the revealed and only salvific Truth always be discernable.

We selected the subject of the present study with this in mind, when we were very honored by the invitation to participate in the "Theological Symposium" sponsored by the "Patriarchal Institute for Patristic Studies," which is under the direction of Prof. Panayiotis Christou. The "Symposium" met from 24–27 August 1981 in Thessaloniki, and the subject was the Second Ecumenical Council.

The first part of the present work, i.e. the Interpretation of Canon VII of the Second Ecumenical Council by the *Kollyvades* and by C. Oikonomos of the Oikonomoi, constituted the report which was read at the "Symposium." It was deemed necessary, however, to supplement the report with the historical dimension of the problem, i.e. the same writers' teaching on the application of this Canon in the life of the Church.

Hence, it is from the bottom of our heart that we thank the P.I.P.S. for providing us with the occasion to compose the present work, and also certain venerable fathers of the Holy Mountain, who not only morally, but also materially contributed to its publication. The sure fact that the Holy Mountain in every age, and particularly today, continues to be the ark in which the Orthodox Holy-Spiritual way of life (hesychastic tradition) is preserved unaltered and the Orthodox Faith remains intact, serves to underline the importance of the *Kollyvades* Fathers of the Holy Mountain —and indeed St. Nikodemos who was surnamed *Hagioritis*, which means "resident of the Holy Mountain"—as bearers and witnesses of Orthodox Tradition.

+ Protopresbyter George D. Metallinos
Epiphany, 1983

PREFACE TO THE ENGLISH EDITION

THE WRITING of this study was occasioned by a specific event relevant to today's interchurch or ecumenical relations and their evident conflict with the authentic ecclesiastical tradition of the Prophets, the Apostles and our Fathers and Mothers throughout the ages. In 1978, I met three German students in Cologne who had already been catechized in the Orthodox tradition. They requested that I assume the task of completing their catechism, and that I "baptize" them Orthodox. This meant that they be received by our Church through the one and authentic baptism performed in the name of the Holy Trinity, with trine immersion and emersion in water.

It being known that the Latins have been called heretics at the Orthodox Church's Eighth Ecumenical Council (Constantinople, 879) because of the *filioque* heresy, and that after the Council of Trident (16th cen.) the canonical baptism has been completely lost in the West and has been replaced by aspersion or affusion, I therefore sought permission from the Archdiocese of Athens for them to be received by the Church of Greece "by *acrivia*." Permission was granted (for this practice had never been abolished in the Church of Greece), and their baptism took place, according to the practice of the early Church, on the night of Holy Saturday, 1979.

When this became known, I was strongly attacked, not only by Latins (in Greece and in W. Germany), but also by Latinizing pro-unionists and Uniates within Greece. This led to the beginning of a verbal struggle in the mass media (press, radio, television), during the course of which I decided to write a theological study on the issue, not in order to justify my action—which had the approval of my Church and, of foremost importance, was consonant with the Orthodox tradition—but to present the relevant Orthodox teaching within the actual practice of my Church.

Hence it was with great joy that I accepted the invitation of the "Patriarchal Institute for Patristic Studies" in Thessaloniki to participate in its August 1981 Conference with the theme the Second Ecumenical Council. For, in treating of that Council's very important Canon VII (and the corresponding Canon XCV of the Penthekte Ecumenical Council), I would have the opportunity to present the interpretation of it by great figures of the Orthodox Church who not only knew the tradition of our Church as few others did, but also lived it.

I believe that this study, which after the Thessaloniki Conference was completed with a chapter on the application of the Canon within the borders of the Romaic Ethnarchy (i.e. the Orthodox world under Ottoman rule), offers a solution to the problem, a solution defended by our patristic tradition and faith. Especially today, it is necessary that we be well acquainted with this tradition, living as we do in the aftermath of the obscuration brought on by the unforgivable haste of certain ecclesiastical personalities on the subject of Ecumenism, and mainly in the area of relations with the Latin Church (which is identical with the "Vatican State"), due to the interference, once again, of purely secular criteria in the so-called "Ecumenical Dialogue." This trend led to the recent decision of the Seventh Plenary Session of the Joint International Commission for the official Theological Dialogue between Catholics and Orthodox (Balamand, Lebanon, 17–24 July 1993). In no uncertain terms, the delegates from the nine Orthodox Churches represented at this meeting (absent were the Churches of Jerusalem, Georgia, Greece, Serbia, Bulgaria, and Czechoslovakia) propose to their Churches the mutual recognition of sacraments, ignoring Ecumenical Councils, dogma, and history, and thus seeking a de facto union with the Papacy.

It is nothing unusual, then, that the Greek-language Uniate newspaper *Katholike* emphasizes paragraph 13 of the Balamand meeting's "Documentation Supplement" which ends as follows: "It is clear that within this framework, *any re-baptism is excluded...*" Of course, the theologically correct response to this is that Orthodox Church, on the basis of her self-understanding, does not *re*-baptize non-Orthodox converts, but canonically *baptizes* them as having never received the one and canonical baptism of the Church. This, anyway, is the response of the writers whose testimony we invoke in the present study. Aside from all this, any chance recognition of Latin sacraments (and primarily of Holy Orders) on our part notwithstanding leads to the rejection of our whole ecclesiology, of the Ecumenical Councils, and, in a word, of patristic theology (on the basis of which there exist no sacraments amongst the Latins who still, in fact, speak about *"gratia creata"*).

We therefore pray that the local Orthodox Churches, with the encouragement surely of the six Churches that did not participate in the aforementioned meeting and did not sign its decisions, not proceed with the acceptance of the proposals of their representatives at Balamand; for otherwise highly unfavorable developments are foreseen that will seriously affect Orthodox unity.

This translation was made on the initiative of a very dear colleague of mine, the Greek-American Priestmonk Fr. Seraphim of St. Paul's Monastery on the Holy Mountain. Apparently his good heart perceived the need today for this study. I thank him from the bottom of my heart; and likewise the venerable Elder and Abbot of his monastery, my respected Fr. Parthenios, a zealous proponent of the Apostolico-patristic tradition, who readily gave his blessing for this translation.

I moreover thank the holy Abbot for the decision that St. Paul's Monastery publish the English edition of this study. My own wholly academic labor cannot compare with their uniquely salvific-experiential witness which they wish to preserve by propounding the teaching of their forerunners, the *Kollyvades*.

+ Protopresbyter George D. Metallinos
Pentecost, 1994

ABBREVIATIONS

E = Neophytos Kafsokalyvitis, *Ἐπιτομὴ τῶν Ἱερῶν Κανόνων* [*Digest of the Sacred Canons*] (unpublished).

P = *Πηδάλιον*... [*The Rudder*], by Agapios Priestmonk and Nikodemos Monk, 8th ed. (Athens, 1976). Cf English translation by D. Cummings (Chicago, 1957), and particularly St. Nikodemos' footnotes and explanations of the relevant Canons. In this study all references to *The Rudder* are cited and translated anew from the 1976 Greek edition.

M = Athanasios Parios, *Ὅτι οἱ ἀπὸ Λατίνων ἐπιστρέφοντες ἀναντιρρήτως, ἀπαραιτήτως καὶ ἀναγηαίως πρέπει νὰ βαπτίζωνται καὶ Ἐπιτομὴ...τῶν θείων τῆς πίστεως δογμάτων*... [*That Latin converts must indisputably, indispensably and necessarily be baptized, and Digest...of the Divine Dogmas of the Faith*] (Leipzig, Saxony, 1806). Excerpts in: Theodoritos Monk Hagioreitis, *Μοναχισμὸς καὶ Αἵρεσις (Monasticism and Heresy)* (Athens, 1977), pp. 263ff.

O = *Τὰ σωζόμενα ἐκκλσιαστικὰ συγγράμματα Κωνσταντίνου Πρεσβυτέρου καὶ Οἰκονόμου τοῦ ἐξ Οἰκονόμων*, ἐκδιδόντος Σοφ. Κ. τοῦ ἐξ Οἰκονόμων, τόμος Α' [*The extant ecclesiastical writings of Constantine Presbyter and Oikonomos of the Oikonomoi*, published by Soph. C. of the Oikonomoi], vol. I (Athens, 1862), pp. 398–515.

Patriarch Cyril V of Constantinople (+1775)

INTRODUCTION

THE DEBATE over the validity of the baptism of non-Orthodox who come over to Orthodoxy, a very old problem of the Church,¹ flared up around the middle of the eighteenth century in the see of the Ecumenical Patriarchate, during the reign of Cyril V² beginning in 1750. The reopening of

1 For the history of the problem see I.N. Karmiris, «Πῶς δεῖ δέξεσθαι τοὺς προσιόντας τῇ Ὀρθοδοξίᾳ ἑτεροδόξους» ["How should non-Orthodox who come over to Orthodoxy be received"], *Τὰ Δογματικὰ καὶ Συμβολικὰ Μνημεῖα τῆς Ὀρθοδόξου Καθολικῆς Ἐκκλησίας* [*The Dogmatic and Symbolic Monuments of the Orthodox Catholic Church*], vol. II (Athens, 1953), pp. 972–1050 (972–1025); T. Ware, *Eustratios Argenti: A Study of the Greek Church under Turkish Rule* (Oxford, 1964), p. 65ff; Evêque Pierre l'Hullier, "Les Divers Modes de Reception des Catholiques-Romains dans l'Orthodoxie," *Le Messager Orthodoxe* 1 (1962), pp. 15–23; J. I. Kotsonis, «Αἱρετικῶν Βάπτισμα» ["Heretical Baptism"], *Θρησκευτικὴ καὶ Ἠθικὴ Ἐγκυκλοπαιδεία* [*Encyclopedia of Religion and Ethics*] 1 (1962), col. 1092-1095; A. Christophilopoulos, «Ἡ εἰς Ὀρθοδοξίαν προσέλευσις τῶν ἀλλοθρήσκων καὶ ἑτεροδόξων» ["The coming to Orthodoxy of non-Christians and non-Orthodox"], *Θεολογία* ΚΖ' (1956), pp. 53–60, 196–205. In these works one may find further bibliography. See also Gerhard Podskalsky, *Griechische Theologie in der Zeit der Türkenherrschaft 1453–1821*, p. 35 (bibliography in n. 96); Cf. Vasileios N. Yiannopoulos, *Ἡ ἀποδοχὴ τῶν αἱρετικῶν κατὰ τήν Z΄ Οἰκουμενικὴν Σύνοδον* [*The Reception of Heretics according to the Seventh Ecumenical Council*] (Athens, 1988) (Reprint from *Θεολογία ΝΘ'* (1988), pp. 530–579). Dorothea Wendeburg, "Taufe und Oikonomia. Zur Furge der Wiedertaufe in der Orthodoxen Kirche," *Kirchengemeinschaft—Anspruch und Wirklichkeit. Festschrift für G. Kretschmar* (Stuttgart, 1986), pp. 93-116. Lothar Heiser, *Die Taufe in der Orthodoxe Kirch (Geschichte, Spedung und Symbolik nach der Lehre der Väter)*, (Trier, 1987).

2 On him see E. Skouvaras, «Στηλιτευτικὰ Κείμενα τοῦ ΙΗ' αἰῶνος (Κατὰ

the problem by this Patriarch, who imposed (re)baptism of Western converts, provoked vehement disputes that survived in print as a very rich production of relevant literature.[3] Hence this issue, together with the *"kollyva* dispute" that broke out around the same time, theologically stamp the eighteenth century, otherwise relatively poor in theological interest.

The question of how the (early) heretics were to be received was synodically resolved by the early Church through, among others, Canon VII of the Second Ecumenical Council.[4] Therefore, it was reasonable that, in the solutions also proposed for regulating the matter in the eighteenth century, an interpretation of this Canon be attempted applying it now to the case of the later heretics, i.e. the Westerners in general, and specifically the Latins.

It was in this perspective that the *Kollyvades* of the Holy Mountain,[5] as offspring of their time, inevitably viewed the

---

Ἀναβαπτιστῶν)» ["Censorious Texts of the Eighteenth Century (Against Rebaptizers)"], *Byzantinisch-Neugriechische Jahrbücher* 20 (1970), pp. 50–227 (also in reprint); see pp. 58-60 for bibliography. Important is the article by T. A. Gritsopoulos, Θ.Η.Ε. 7 (1965), col. 1193–1197. Cf. same author, «Ὁ Πατριάρχης Κ/λεως Κύριλλος Ε' ὁ Καράκαλλος» ["Patriarch of Constantinople Cyril V Karakallos"], *Ε.Ε.Β.Σ.* ΚΘ' (1959), pp. 367–389.

3   Collected in the above-mentioned work by E. Skouvaras. For the synodal and theological material see J. D. Mansi, *Sacrorum Conciliorum Nova et Amplissima Collectio* 38 (Graz, 1961; Paris, 1907), col. 575–634.

4   Canon XCV of Penthekte is but a reiteration of it. For the text of this canon, see Appendix I.

5   See Ch. S. Tzogas, *Ἡ περὶ μνημοσύνων ἔρις ἐν Ἁγίῳ Ὄρει κατὰ τὸν ιή αἰῶνα* [*The Memorial-service Dispute on the Holy Mountain in the Eighteenth Century*] (Thessaloniki, 1969), with extensive bibliography; C. C. Papoulidis, *Τὸ κίνημα τῶν Κολλυβάδων* [*The "Kollyvades" Movement*] (Athens, 1971); same author, "Nikodème l'Hagiorite (1749-1809)," Θεολογία ΛΖ' (1966), pp. 293–313, 390–415, 576–590, and ΛΗ' (1967), pp. 95–118, 301–311; same author, «Περίπτωσις πνευματικῆς ἐπιδράσεως τοῦ Ἁγίου Ὄρους εἰς τὸν βαλκανικὸν χῶρον κατὰ τὸν ΙΗ' αἰῶνα» ["A case of spiritual influence on the Balkans by the Holy Mountain during the eighteenth century"], *Μακεδονικά* 9 (1969), pp. 278–294; Ch. G. Sotiropoulos, *Κολλυβάδες— Ἀντικολλυβάδες* [*Kollyvades and Anti-Kollyvades*] (Athens, 1981).

Canon in question, the most fundamental for the problem. Being contemporaries of the dispute over the baptism of non-Orthodox,[6] these very capable theologians lived it from up close, and they took a position on it in their writings, offering a solution to the problem that was in accordance with their own theological principles. Neophytos Kafsokalyvitis[7] the leader of the *Kollyvades* movement, St. Nikodemos of the Holy Mountain,[8] and Athanasios Parios,[9] in absolute agreement with each other, unreservedly sided in favor of Patriarch Cyril's decision and the theology of Eustratios Argentis (1687–1757),[10] who defined the theological and canonical frame of reference of the problem in a systematic and decisive way. The above-mentioned

---

6   In the course of explaining Apostolic Canon XLVI, after a lengthy note on the validity of heretical baptism, St. Nikodemos characteristically remarks: "All this theory which we did here is not superfluous, but indeed very necessary, simply for all times, but much more today because of the big debate and great controversy going on over Latin baptism, not only between us and the Latins, but also between us and the Latinizers." *P*, p. 55.

7   See Tzogas, pp. 16–28; Papoulidis, *The "Kollyvades" Movement*, pp. 30–32; Theodoritos Monk (Ioannis Mavros), *Νεοφύτον Ἱεροδιακόνον Καυσοκαλυβίτον, Περί τῆς συνεχοῦς Μεταλήψεως, Εἰσαγωγή, Κείμενον ἀνέκδοτον, Σχόλια* [*Neophytos Deacon-Monk Kafsokalyvitis, On Frequent Communion, Introduction, Unpublished Text, Commentary*]. (Athens, n.d.); A. Camariano-Cioran, *Les Académies princières du Bucarest et de Jassy et leurs professeurs* (Thessaloniki, 1974), pp. 413–431.

8   See Tzogas, pp. 46–51; Papoulidis, *The "Kollyvades" Movement*, pp. 35–37; and the other works cited in n. 5 above. Also important is the monograph by Fr. Theocletos, Monk of the Monastery of Dionysiou (Holy Mountain), *Ἅγιος Νικόδημος ὁ Ἁγιορείτης* [*Saint Nikodemos of the Holy Mountain*] (Athens, 1959). See also George S. Bebis, "St. Nikodemos the Hagiorite," in *Post-Byzantine Ecclesiastical Personalities*, pp. 1–17; Podskalsky, pp. 377–382 (with extensive bibliography); C. Cavarnos, *St. Nicodemos the Hagiorite: An Account of his Life, Character and Message, together with a Comprehensive List of his Writing and Selections from Them* (Belmont, MA: 1974; 2nd ed. 1979).

9   See Tzogas, pp. 29–43; Papoulidis, *The "Kollyvades" Movement*, pp. 37–39; Podskalsky, pp. 358–365 (with bibliography).

10 Ware, p. 90ff; Podskalsky, pp. 331–335 (bibliography).

Kollyvades,[11] each in his own peculiar way, affirm[12] and reiterate

---

11 We took into account the following works of theirs, in which their relevant teaching is presented:

a. Neophytos Kafsokalyvitis, Ἐπιτομὴ τῶν Ἱερῶν Κανόνων *(Digest of the Sacred Canons)*, Characterized by Tzogas as "famous" (p. 26), and composed of 1227 pages of unequal size. It remains yet unpublished in MS 222 (=295) of the Academy of Bucharest, fol. 2a–1227. See C. Litzica, *Catalogul Manuscriptelor Grecesti* (Bucuresti, 1909), p. 150. Cf Theodoritos Monk, «'Ο Νομοκάνων Νεοφύτου τοῦ Καυσοκαλυβίτου» ["The Code of Church Laws and Canons by Neophytos Kafsokalyvitis"], *Κοινωνία* IH' (1975), pp. 197–206. Fr. Theodoritos has prepared the critical edition of this work, and he very kindly made available to us a section of it containing the chapters: 1) "On those coming over to Orthodoxy," p. 126–147 xvii, and 2) "On Canon Seven of the Second Ecumenical Council and Ninety-five of the Sixth" (fol. 147xx–147xxv), and therefore we express to him our thank and gratitude. Fr. Theodoritos accepts that this work was written while the author resided on the Holy Mountain, i.e. before 1759 (see *On Frequent Communion*, p. 33), and he completed it with later additions until his death (1784). A part of the above-mentioned first chapter (pages 126–127 and 147–148 of the work) was published in his book *M (Monasticism and Heresy)*, pp. 254–257. It is clear from Neophytos' work that he knew well the arguments of Cyril V's opponents. We follow the numbering of the MS used by Fr. Theodoritos (the Greek numerals being replaced by Roman numerals).

b. Nikodemos Monk (Hagioritis), *Πηδάλιον* [*The Rudder*], 1st ed. (Leipzig, 1800). Herein we have in mind the 8th ed. (Athens, 1976). According to the in-depth scholar of the saint's works, Fr. Theocletos, Monk of Dionysiou, *The Rudder* "is entirely the work of the Saint," (op. cit., pp. 214–215). In many places in *The Rudder*, St. Nikodemos refers to Canon VII of the Second Ecumenical Council, particularly in the *ad hoc* interpretation of it and of Canon XCV of Penthekte.

c. Athanasios Parios, Ἐπιτομὴ τῶν θείων τῆς πίστεως δογμάτων [*Digest of the Divine Dogmas of the Faith*] (Leipzig, Saxony, 1806). See a small section of this work in *M*. pp. 265–268. Athanasios Parios also wrote a special concise study titled, «Ὅτι οἱ ἀπὸ Λατίνων ἐπισρέγοντες ἀναντιρρήτως, ἀπαραιτήτως καὶ ἀναγκαίως πρέπει νὰ βαπτίζονται» ["That Latin converts must indisputably, indispensably and necessarily be baptized"], which survives in cod. 88 of the Holy Monastery of Xenophontos, pp. 394–397, and was published by Fr. Theodoritos, *M*, pp. 263–265. For an excerpt of this, see Appendix V.

12 Our theologians were aware of Argentis' work, Ἐγχειρίδιον περὶ βαπτίσματος [*Handbook on Baptism*], 1st ed. (Constantinople, 1756), and 2nd ed. (Leipzig, 1757), and they even refer to it: Nikodemos, *P*, pp. 35–36, 55; A. Parios, *M*, p. 266; and *O*, p. 511. Neophytos cites the decision of Cyril V, *E*, p. 147xxv.

Argentis' view and solution of the problem, and thus uphold the Church's early practice as canonically formulated by Sts. Cyprian of Carthage and Basil the Great. Also, the fact that the Priestmonk Jonas,[13] one of Patriarch Cyril V's most active co-workers in Constantinople and himself a "rebaptizer," was also a *Kafsokalyvitis*, i.e. a fellow monastic of Neophytos, should not, in my opinion, remain unnoticed. Perhaps the Athonite society, and in this case Neophytos, was more significantly involved in this problem than has been known until now. But for the time being, this is but a mere guess which is worthy, however, of further investigation.

Around the middle of the nineteenth century, Constantine Oikonomos of the Oikonomoi was called upon to confront this very same problem theologically, the occasion being the important Palmer affair.[14] In three lengthy epistolary dissertations[15]—a favorite custom of his— Oikonomos attempted a detailed theological analysis of the

13 See Skouvaras, pp. 68–71.

14 Oikonomos was called upon by A. Stourzas, residing in Russia, to take a position on the problem raised by the case of the renowned Scottish deacon William Palmer, who so wearied both the Russian Church and the Ecumenical Patriarchate. With this opportunity he wrote the studies listed below. See *O*, pp. 498, 494. On Palmer see Ware, pp. 103–104 (bibliography), and Georges Florovsky, *Aspects of Church History* (Belmont, 1975), pp. 227–238; bibliography, pp. 305–306 (n. 23–26).

15 These are: 1) Notes to the anonymous dissertation "on the rite of the sacrament of Holy Baptism," (1 March, 1850); 2) An excerpt from a letter to A. Stourzas on the same issue (2 March, 1847); and 3) A Letter to a Bishop (30 Dec. 1852). These are published in *O*. pp. 398–485, 486–492, and 493–515 respectively. Oikonomos also deals with the subject of the baptism of heretics in his study: Περὶ τῶν τριῶν Ἱερατικῶν τῆς Ἐκκλησίας βαθμῶν Ἐπιστολιμαία Διατριβή, ἐν ᾗ καὶ περὶ τῆς γνησιότητος τῶν Ἀποστολικῶν κανόνων, ὑπὸ τοῦ Πρεσβυτέρου καὶ Οἰκονόμου Κωσταντίνου τοῦ ἐξ Οἰκονόμων [*Epistolary Dissertation on the Church's three Sacerdotal Orders, and also on the authenticity of the Apostolic Canons, by Constantine Presbyter and Oikonomos of the Oikonomoi*], (Nauplia, 1835), pp. 131–139, and 144–152 (on Apostolic Canons XLVI, XLVII and L). But what is said here is also included in his above-listed studies.

problem, taking up the position of Cyril V and E. Argentis, and hence also that of the *Kollyvades*.[16] He interprets Canon VII of the Second Ecumenical Council on the basis of the same presuppositions and thinking as they, in order to apply it to Western converts. That is to say that in the case of both the *Kollyvades* and Oikonomos the interpretation of the Canon is not undertaken without presuppositions, but is inseparably interwoven with its application to the later heretics.

Thus, the effort is made by these theologians to preserve the continuity of the Church's tradition, and to express the Orthodox conscience in their own time. Moving within the same spiritual climate, and being theologically well equipped, especially as regards canon law, they make a significant contribution to the treatment of a problem that continues to concern the Church to this day. Their contribution lies not so much in the originality of their interpretation (for essentially they reiterate the theology of Argentis), but in their personal recasting and re-expression of the Church's tradition. Though in a form imposed by the necessity for a detailed confrontation of the argumentation of those who thought otherwise,[17] their response cannot fail to be taken seriously in whatever synodal settlement of the issue may

---

16 Oikonomos was aware of the existence of Neophytos' *Digest*, and he praises the work in vol. IV of his own monumental work, Περὶ τῶν Ο' Ἑρμηνευτῶν τῆς Π. θείας Γραφῆς [*On the Seventy Translators of the Old Testament*], p. 821. Cf. Tzogas, p. 71. In the same work he praises Athanasios Parios and St. Nikodemos of the Holy Mountain (p. 822). In his above-mentioned texts, he uses *The Rudder* (1841 edition) and cites it by name (e.g., pp. 400, 417, 511: "…the most ascetic Nikodemos of the Holy Mountain (in *The Rudder*, p. 31)." He does not hesitate, though, to criticize it. E.g. on p. 460 n., he notes: "And see the inconsistent and wavering remarks in *The Rudder*, p. 16" (of the 2nd ed., 1841).

17 As for the *Kollyvades*, we have ascertained that they are aware of the argumentation developed in the texts of the metropolitans et al. written in opposition to the decision of Ecumenical Patriarch Cyril V. See Mansi 38.

come about, inasmuch as this is demanded by the authority the *Kollyvades* as well as C. Oikonomos carry in our Church, all possible objections aside.[18] The manner employed by the aforementioned writers in dealing with the problem may very well clearly reek of scholasticism and hence naturally be repulsive to modern Greek theological thought, which day by day is becoming less and less scholastic. Yet when placed in the framework of their time, it is more easily understood. Moreover, it also helps us in approaching similar problems in our own time.

It goes without saying that the present work is mainly a study of literature and canon law, but also a parallel study of moral obligation.

---

18 Opinions on the *Kollyvades* are often contradictory. One may ascertain this from studying the above-named works by Ch. Tzogas on the one hand, and the studies by Theocletos, Monk of Dionysiou, and C. Papoulidis on the other. And even Prof. P. Christou portrays St. Nikodemos as "often wavering between extreme conservatism and extreme modernism," emphatically stating: "The canonization [of the *Kollyvades*] did not also impose the recognition of their views on the disputed issues." See P. C. Christou, «Τὸ Ἅγιον Ὄρος ἐν τῷ παρελθόντι καὶ τῷ παρόντι» ["The Holy Mountain, Past and Present"], *Ἀθωνικὴ Πολιτεία* (Thessaloniki, 1963), pp. 64–65. We believe that above scholarly opinion is the conscience of the Church at large, which holds the *Kollyvades* in high esteem, whereas, on the contrary, their opponents it has condemned, at least to oblivion!

CHAPTER I
The Principal Figures

1. The "*Kollyvades*" Fathers of the Holy Mountain

THE APPEARANCE in the eighteenth century of the *Kollyvades* on the Holy Mountain, and in Greece in general, constitutes a dynamic return to the roots of Orthodox tradition, to the "philokalic" experience which is at the core of the Orthodox Church's spirituality. Their "movement," as it was called, was regenerative and traditional, progressive and yet patristic. In other words, genuinely Orthodox. Using the scholarly methods of the time (composing writings), they first of all revealed the continuity of hesychasm on the Holy Mountain Athos, and at the same time remained faithful not only to the theoretical formulation of the hesychastic-Palamite theology, but also to its practical applications, i.e. the whole spectrum of the ascetic experience. Through the dissemination of their works and by their struggles in defense of the tradition, they formed the counterbalance against the European "Enlightenment," and in their own right became enlighteners of their Nation and of Orthodoxy at large.

That is why they were loved by traditionalists, but hated and fought (or slandered) by those who were instilled with the spirit of Frankish scholasticism or of the Anglo-French Enlightenment and were thus cut off from the philokalic roots. The hypertrophic (metaphysical) rationalism of the westernizers, a standing threat to the patristic way of theology, thus proved to be foreign to the experiential and Holy-spiritual way of theology which the *Kollyvades* Fathers embodied and preached. If our reconnection with the genuine, theological tradition of the Fathers has been achieved in our day, this is owed to the precursory labors of the *Kollyvades*.

A contingent of Athonite monks in the second half of the eighteenth century, living within the tradition of "noetic prayer" or "prayer of the heart," and being provoked by a seemingly insignificant happening, which, however, had deep theological roots and enormous extensions, will light the Church's course and reveal the continuity or discontinuity of the fullness of Orthodoxy. The monk of St. Anne's Skete on the Holy Mountain were building a larger church and, since they wanted to be able to work on Saturdays in order to complete it, they decided to move the memorial services from Saturday to Sunday after the Divine Liturgy. This decision, which conflicted with the Church's practice and theology (Sunday being the day of the Resurrection is a day of joy), scandalized the deacon Neophytos the Peloponnesian of the nearby Skete of Kafsokalyvia, who was the first to rise up with a theological campaign against the decision of the monks of St. Anne's. One further event also served to intensify the now ignited flame. In 1777, a book advocating the necessity of "frequent Holy Communion" was published from among the circle of Athonite hesychasts who, because of their involvement in the dispute "concerning memorial services" were by their opponents collectively called *Kollyvades* (from *kollyva*, the boiled wheat used at memorial services). The book was condemned by the Ecumenical Patriarchate in 1785, for it supposedly created scandals and dissensions. Aside from exposing the contra-traditional attitude of the monks of St. Anne's, this action revealed how Orthodox criteria had become obscured, thus affirming, also for Greece, what the ever-memorable Fr. Georges Florovsky called "pseudomorphosis." The Patriarchate's later decision, moreover, by which the condemnation was lifted, serves to show the instability of these matters.

The men who advocated the canonical performance of memorial services on Saturday also advocated frequent Holy Communion (when, of course, the correct Orthodox presuppositions of an ongoing spiritual life exists), thus ranging the practice of the early Church against the unfounded actions of their opponents. The latter, being as they were completely estranged from the tradition of the holy Fathers, accused the *Kollyvades* of being innovators, in exactly the same way that the fourteenth century Scholastics (Nicephorus Gregoras, John Kyparissiotes, et al.) had accused the hesychasts of the Holy Mountain of being "modernists." But then, the case of the *Kollyvades* is only a repetition of the affair of the hesychasts of the fourteenth century; for both groups, each in its own way, stood up against the spirit of the estranged West and against the westernizing of the "unionists" and westernizers of the East. The *Kollyvades* emphasized the issue of worship, for they diagnosed that there, i.e. in the area of the spirituality that preserved the unity of the subjugated Orthodox people, the problem of estrangement was perceptible. They encouraged participation in the sacraments of the Church accompanied by a parallel spiritual struggle. They strove for the correct observance of the Church's typicon that would maintain the spiritual balance, and for the study of patristic works that would cultivate a patristic, i.e. the Church's, mind. That is why the honor belongs to the *Kollyvades*, in that they preserved the Apostolico-patristic continuity in the Church: noetic prayer and hesychastic practice, asceticism and experience, those enduring and unalterable elements of the Orthodox identity.

This contingent of Athonite hesychasts (*Kollyvades*) had their leaders, three of whom are among the theologians dealt with in the present study. Namely they are the following:

1) Neophytos Kafsokalyvitis (1713–1784), from 1749 rector of Athonias School on the Holy Mountain, is the man who initiated the cause; but after his expulsion from the Holy Mountain, he discontinued his active participation in the *Kollyvades* "movement" for reasons unknown. He dealt mainly with education, serving as rector in Chios around 1760; in Adrianoupolis in 1763; and in what is today Rumania, Bucharest 1767, Bravsko 1770, and from 1773 until his death again in Bucharest. He left behind a number of important works, among which are some on canon law.

2) Saint Makarios (1731–1805), a descendant of the renowned Byzantine family of Notaras, was born in Corinth and later became Metropolitan of the diocese of Corinthia (1765-1769). He was the "animater" of the movement and the person who not only encouraged St. Nikodemos to write, but also supplied him with material for his works. He died on 16 April 1805 on the island of Chios where he was living at the time, and the people immediately honored him as a saint.

3) Saint Nikodemos of the Holy Mountain (1749–1809), officially declared a saint in 1955, was the "theologian" of the *Kollyvades* contingent. A great hesychast-ascetic and a highly accomplished author of patristic caliber, he left behind a multitude of writings in which the whole patristic tradition is recast. One who studies the works of St. Nikodemos can unreservedly say that he has gone through patristic theology in its entirety. His *Handbook of Counsel* is, for modern times, the representative work on Orthodox spirituality. The publication of the multivolume *Philokalia of the Wakeful Fathers* (in collaboration with St. Makarios, but essentially the work of Nikodemos) contributed to spiritual rebirth in Orthodox countries. His work *The Rudder* constitutes the most authoritative compilation of our Church's holy Canons and explanations of them in conjunction with the Church's spirituality.[19]

---

19 Ed. This is confirmed in St. Nikodemos' day and in subsequent generations. However, in recent years an argument has been put forward and gained some acceptance that there was conflict between St. Nikodemos and Dorotheos Voulismas (who represented the Ecumenical Patriarchate as "teacher" of the Great Church). This peculiar theory was proposed by Professor Theodore Yangou in Greece and eventually became known to the English-speaking world also. To set the record straight again, Archimandrite Nikodemos Barousis led the publication of an 800-page tome providing the correspondences between St. Nikodemos of the Holy Mountain and Dorotheos Voulismas, but he also included other letters too, for example, letters between more saints of the day and the patriarch. Archimandrite Nicodemos thus gives us the whole context of their discussions (See Οἱ Κολλυβάδες καὶ ὁ Δωρόθεος Βουλησμᾶς. Τὸ ζήτημα τῆς ἀνακρίσεως τοῦ Πηδαλίου καὶ τοῦ Κανονικοῦ [*The Kollyvades and Dorotheus Boulesmas: The Question of the Examination of the Pedalion and of the Canonicon*], Tenos: Athens 2020 [in Greek]). Yangou misrepresents Voulismas and therefore the Ecumenical Patriarchate as standing against St. Nikodemos. They claim St. Nikodemos was forced by Patriarch Neophytos to edit the text of *The Rudder* to adhere to the beliefs of Voulismas where their teachings supposedly were in conflict; then they implied *The Rudder* would not be published unless St. Nikodemos submitted to their will. However, Archimandrite Nikodemos Barousis demonstrates the historical truth that Voulismas and St. Nikodemos were united in their stance on how to pastorally use *economia*. Their letters illustrate simply a discussion on this and also how *economia* was applied historically. Many letters have Voulismas deferring to St. Nikodemos and his requests, wishes, and (importantly) to the saint's desire that *The Rudder* be a book which "belongs to the Church" and not a book of his own making and beliefs. Both St. Nikodemos of the Holy Mountain and Dorotheos Voulismas of Constantinople were both principled and holy men. They had their own writings which supported the patristic revival of the Kollyvades Fathers in their time. The fact of the matter is that Constantinople and these saints were collaborators and *The*

4) Athanasios Parios (1722–1813) was the most militant of the *Kollyvades*, and also the most martyric. From 1776 to 1781 he remained unfrocked as a "heretic" because of his vigorous stand on the issues of tradition. He passionately fought the European Enlightenment, Voltaireanism, and atheism, and was accused of being an obscurantist by his "West-struck" contemporaries. He, however, was not fighting education which he himself served, nor even the exact sciences themselves; but rather the "godless letters" and the conceit of the wisdom of this world (cf. Jas. 3:15). A prolific author, he left behind numerous writings full of patristic wisdom and spirituality.

The *Kollyvades* exerted a tremendous influence in their day, but also on the generations that followed. Their influence initially was greater off the Holy Mountain than on it. Today, however, the Holy Mountain acknowledges their contribution to the rebirth of Orthodox spirituality and follows their tradition. In spite of the fact that the *Antikollyvades* by far outnumbered the *Kollyvades* and engaged in a systematic persecution of them, not only did they fail to frustrate the latter's effort, but they in fact contributed to the spreading of their spirit in Greece and in the other Orthodox countries (Transdanubian regions, Russia, etc).

Rudder was published as a book of the Church and not any one individual or group within the Church.

In subsequent generations, this is confirmed. St. Raphael (Hawaweeny) of Brooklyn (who had broad experiences in the Middle East, Russia, and North America) is a significant witness. St. Raphael mentioned anyone presenting Orthodoxy "...must resort to official books that are assuredly published, officially endorsed, and acknowledged by all the Orthodox Churches, such as The Collection of all the Canons of the Apostles, the Ecumenical Councils, the Local Councils, and the Fathers of the Church called *Pedalion* in Greek (meaning *The Rudder*) that was printed upon the request of the Patriarch and the Synod of the Church of Constantinople and is acknowledged by all the Orthodox Churches of the East" (Hawaweeny, St. Raphael, *In Defense of Saint Cyprian*, (Florence, AZ: Uncut Mountain Press, 2023), pp. 17, 19).

To the *Kollyvades* is owed the rebirth of hesychasm in the nineteenth century. Even today, the *Kollyvades* Fathers continue to be spiritual guides for the Orthodox, and the principal bridge of reconnection with the patristic tradition. The rediscovery of the hesychasm of the fourteenth century, and chiefly of its champion St. Gregory Palamas (d. 1357), was accomplished thanks to the seeds that the *Kollyvades* of the eighteenth century sowed.

Bibliography

See Introduction above, n. 5–8.

2. Constantine Oikonomos of the Oikonomoi (1780–1857)

Greece's most notable cleric and theologian of the nineteenth century, C. Oikonomos, was occupied with the work of education. Initially he taught in Smyrna (1809–1819), at the same time preaching and contending against the propaganda of the non-Orthodox missionaries. He was made a *Great Oikonomos* of the Ecumenical Patriarchate and *Preacher General of the Great Church of Christ* by the Hieromartyr Ecumenical Patriarch Gregory V[20] (d. 1821). After the outbreak of the Greek Revolution in 1821, he fled to Odessa in Russia where there was a significant Greek community. The Czars on several occasions honored him with decorations and monetary rewards, and finally with a life pension (7000 rubles annually). The Academy of Berlin proclaimed him a corresponding member thereof, and

---

20 This same Patriarch Gregory the V responded favorably to the efforts of St. Nikodemos the Hagiorite when asked to receive a blessing to baptize a Latin. See the text of this letter in Appendix IV.

Chapter I: The Principal Figures 33

he became known in Europe for his many and important writings.

In October 1834 he returned to the newly established Greek State, and in 1837 he settled permanently in Athens where, until his death, he was active as a scholar, author, private teacher, and ecclesiastical orator. His home became a center for the more important educated men of the time, and he taught a multitude of spiritual children who eventually held important positions in Greek society and the Church. He strove against the Western missionaries and their activities against the Church, and likewise against anti-Church activities of the Greek State.

C. Oikonomos was the principal opponent of the *coup d' état* autocephaly of the Church of Greece (the work of the Bavarians in 1833), which, by the forceful severing of the Church of Greece from the Ecumenical Patriarchate which at that time was also the Ethnarchic Center of the Orthodox countries in the Balkans, signaled the beginning of the Western Powers' dissolution of the "Romaic Ethnarchy." Oikonomos was in favor, however, of the canonical proclamation of Greek autocephaly (something achieved in 1850 through his involvement), so that the spiritual ties of the Orthodox peoples of the Ottoman Empire with their Spiritual and Ethnarchic Center be preserved. He maintained relationships and correspondence with the more important figures of his time, in Greece and abroad, and he was the friend of many non-Orthodox scholars, such as the German C. Tischendorf.

He died on 8 March 1857, leaving behind a great wealth of writings, both theological and philological, besides massive correspondence. C. Oikonomos was a researcher of and prime expert on the patristic tradition which he vigorously defended in his writings and in his struggles, according to the challenges of his time, focusing on canonical order and on his rebuttals provoked by the Western ecclesiastical and political propaganda. One target of his rebuttal was the likewise great Greek theologian and scholar cleric Theocletos Pharmakides (1784–1860), who in free Greece represented the Western spirit (in that he had Protestant leanings and was a supporter of British policy).

Bibliography

Papaderos, Alexandros. *Metakenosis: Griechenlands kulturelle Herausforderung durch die Aufklärung in der Sicht des Korais und des Oikonomos.* Meisenheim am Glan: 1970 (also for older bibliography).

Patsavos, Lewis J. "Konstantinos Oikonomos of the Oikonomoi." In *Post-Byzantine Ecclesiastical Personalities*, edited by Nomikos Michael Vaporis, 69–85. Brookline, MA: 1978.

Protopresbyter George D. Metallinos. *Ελλαδικού Αυτοκεφάλου Παραλειπόμενα* (*Overlooked Aspects of the Greek Autocephaly*), 2nd ed. Athens: 1989, (p. 123ff).

3. Cyril V, Patriarch of Constantinople
(Sept. 1748–June 1751; and Sept. 1752–Jan. 1757)

Patriarch Cyril V, who lived in very troubled times, occupies a prominent place in the history of the Ecumenical Patriarchate. Born in the Peloponnesian city of Dimitsana toward the end of the seventeenth century, he lived for a time on the Holy Mountain and on Patmos where he studied and was tonsured a monk. In 1737 he was elected Metropolitan of Melenoikon in Macedonia, and in 1745 was transferred to the diocese of Nicomedia in Asia Minor. In 1748 he was elected Ecumenical Patriarch but was dethroned in 1751 because of disturbances. Already in his first term as patriarch he came into conflict with the Westerners and

Latin propaganda. The French ambassador was his chief opponent, given that France was the protectress of the Latins within the Ottoman Empire.

During his two terms as patriarch, Cyril confronted two fundamental issues, on account of which he acquired many friends, but also many enemies. In order to confront the factionalism of the bishops residing in Constantinople and the continual change of patriarchs which the foreign propaganda took advantage of, he dismissed the residing bishops in 1751 (a measure repeated in 1755), and obliged them to return to their dioceses. Thus he incurred the hatred of many hierarchs and their permanent opposition. This will become apparent primarily over the question of the (re)baptism of Latins. He likewise devoted attention to the finances of the Great Church, conducting collections of funds and, in 1755, forming a mixed committee composed of lay officials and bishops. He also sought to organize education, and to this end founded the Athonias school in 1749.

The question of the (re)baptism of converts from the West is connected with Cyril's efforts, beginning in 1749, to guard Orthodoxy from her increasingly closer embrace with the Latin Church, and to repulse the Pope's proselytistic activities as well as his encroachment on the Shrines in the Holy Lands and on the Patriarchate of Alexandria. He commenced his antipapal campaign, having as he did the trust and cooperation of a major portion of the monks and populace. It was met with indifference from the educated and higher clergy, however, and with opposition from the synodal bishops for the aforementioned reasons.

On 28 April 1755, the synodal bishops convoked a Council in which they censured the book, *A Denunciation of Sprinkling*, and denounced the (re)baptism of Westerners. This counter-effort was spearheaded by Cyril's chief opponent and successor, Callinicus IV. Cyril, for his part, being guided by his patristic mind, and furthermore in order to check Western propaganda which had become overbold, did not hesitate to oppose the body of hierarchs and to condemn their uncanonical action. Thus, in June 1755 he published a response, known by the title "Anathema of those who accept papal sacraments," that was read aloud in the churches and was received with enthusiasm by the pious Orthodox populace. Cyril exposed the pressures he was experiencing to sign the pro-West decision of the hierarchs, and he thus placed in danger not only his throne, but also his life. Yet Cyril also reacted in a more affirmative manner. He dissolved the anti-patriarchal synod and sent the bishops to their dioceses. Then, together with Matthew and Parthenios, the Patriarchs of Alexandria and Jerusalem respectively, he signed the notorious "*Oros* of the Holy Great Church of Christ," which decree recommended "the God-given holy baptism," and scorned "the baptisms otherwise administered by heretics." *His* Oros *constitutes the authorized practice of the Great Church on this question officially in force to this day.*

The traditionalist Patriarch had as an ardent partner in his struggles, among others, the well-known, outstanding theologian of the time, Eustratios Argentis.[21] His enemies did not succeed in reversing the *Oros*, despite their organized opposition, which even included satire and libel. The counteractions against Cyril ultimately led to his dethronement, despite the reactions of the populace which

---

21 Ed. Among others who supported Patriarch Cyril V of Constantinople was his spiritual father, St. Auxentios of Mount Katirli (+1757), a great ascetic and miracle-worker who preached many public sermons on the need for all converts to be received by baptism and in support of the 1755 *Oros*. See An Orthodox Ethos Publication, *On the Reception of the Heterodox into the Orthodox Church: The Patristic Consensus and Criteria*, (Florence, AZ: Uncut Mountain Press, 2023), pp. 296–297.

Chapter I: The Principal Figures   37

remained loyal to the hesychast Patriarch. Two synodal unfrockings were pronounced against him (Jan. 1757, and 1763), which display his enemies' hatred for him, and which constitute real libel. On 27 July 1775, he died on the Holy Mountain, where he was in quiet retirement.

Bibliography

See n. 2 above.

CHAPTER II

Interpretation of the Canon

1. Ecclesiological and Canonical Presuppositions

IN ORDER to understand the manner in which our writers view the Canon in question, we must stay with their presuppositions which are the fruit of the spiritual level of the time, on the one hand, and of their theology, on the other. The theological thought of these theologians moves within the framework of the following ecclesiological and canonical presuppositions:

a) The absolute center around which their theological conscience is formed is Eph. 4:5: "One Lord, one faith, one baptism," and, consequently, One Church, within which alone are the sacraments valid and redemptive. This Church is the Orthodox Church, their Church.[22] In other words, they clearly follow the ecclesiology of St. Cyprian

---

22 *P*, pp. 51, 57. *E*, pp. 139, 142, 147 xiii-xiv (one baptism in the one Church). *O*, pp. 485, 499, 511.

Chapter II: Interpretation of the Canon 39

of Carchedon-Carthage,[23] which, moreover, the entire Orthodox East followed as a rule,[24] in contrast with the West which, here too, followed Augustine.

b) The Apostolic Canons (XLVI, XLVII, L, and LXVIII) which definitively regulate the sacrament of baptism have preeminent and indisputable authority. These theologians do not simply accept that the Apostolic Canons belong to the Church, but also that they are genuinely Apostolic,[25] from which authenticity proceeds their increased authority in the Church. Thus, these Canons are always listed before every other group of Canons, given that both the Canons of the Councils (Ecumenical and Local) as well as those of the holy Fathers are in agreement with them,[26] being as they are of fundamental importance for the life of the Church. As regards baptism, according to our writers, the decision of the Council presided over by Cyprian in 258 was based on the aforementioned Apostolic Canons. And this decision gained Ecumenical authority by its "ratification" by Canon II of the Penthekte Council.[27,28] Therefore, there can be no

---

23 Letters 73:21 and 69:1, 2, 10; 11 Cf. Tertullian, *De baptismo* 15.

24 See Ware, p. 82.

25 According to Neophytos (*E*, p. 132), through them speaks "the assembly of the Apostles"; cf. pp. 131, 132, 133, "the greatest of all Councils, that of the Apostles," *E*, pp. 143–144. See *P.* pp. xxiv, 53, 55. *O*, pp. 399, 452–453, 480. During Oikonomos' time, the Chancellor of the Diocese of Argos, E. Diogeneidis, attacked the authority of the Apostolic Canons. See G. D. Metallinos, *Τὸ ζήτημα τῆς Μεταφράσεως τῆς Ἁγίας Γραφῆς εἰς τὴν Νεοελληνικὴν κατὰ τὸν ΙΘ' αἰῶνα* [*The question of the Translation of Holy Scripture into Modern Greek in the Nineteenth Century*], (Athens, 1977), p. 394. Oikonomos refuted him through the special study mentioned above *(On the Church's three Sacerdotal Orders…)*.

26 *P*, p. 55. *O*, pp. 453–454.

27 *E*, pp. 128, 142. *P*, pp. 51, 370–371. *O*, p. 453. Neophytos declares: "I would sooner depart from my soul than from the incontestable order that the Council of Carchedon-Carthage laid down" (p. 142).

28 Ed. The Penthekte Council is also sometimes referred to as the Fifth-Sixth,

decision of the Church opposed to the Apostolic Canons, the Canon of St. Cyprian, or even those of St. Basil the Great (I and XLVII), which, by virtue of Canon II of Penthekte, have also acquired Ecumenical authority.[29]

c) More specifically with regard to the sacrament of baptism, in accordance with Eph. 4:5 and the Creed, there exists one and only *one* baptism, the baptism of the One Church, i.e. the Orthodox Church.[30] This one is a "baptism" properly speaking, performed by three immersions and emersions, inasmuch as the term βάπτισμα can mean only this.[31] Baptism by trine immersion is "taught by God" and "God-given";[32] this is confirmed by the Apostolic, synodal and patristic Canons.[33] "It is in this baptism that we believe," remarks Oikonomos, "and this is the only one baptism that we confess, never to be repeated."[34]

Quinisext, Trullo, or just the Sixth Ecumenical Council.

29 *E*, pp. 142, 147a–147b. *P*, p. 52. *O*, pp. 426, 451. *M*, p. 263.

30 *P*, p. 51. According to Neophytos: "Well, then, if our baptism and that of heretics is one and the same, then our faith and theirs is also one, even as there is one Lord. But in fact our faith and theirs are not one, and therefore neither is baptism, even as the Lord is not with them" *E*, p. 142. Cf. *O*, pp. 441, 454ff, 485. Oikonomos speaks about "Orthodox baptism." Heretical sacraments are, according to him, "ineffectual" (p. 459).

31 Βαπτίζω, from βάπτω (Mod. Gr. Βουτῶ, i.e. dip, dunk). *O*, p. 402. Oikonomos refutes at length the arguments of his opponents (p. 398ff). Cf. pp. 436ff, 442ff. *P*, p. 63ff. And according to A. Parios (*M*, p. 266), baptism means "to submerse in water the person being baptized."

32 *O*, pp. 399, 426. Cf. p. 413: "all-holy and true." According to the Ecumenical Councils, "the trine immersion and emersion constitutes the conformity to the Lord's command and signifies the triune nature of God." John Rinne (Archbishop of Finland), Ἑνότης καὶ ὁμοιομορφία ἐν τῇ Ἐκκλησίᾳ κατὰ τὸ πνεῦμα τῶν Οἰκουμενικῶν Συνόδων [*Unity and Uniformity in the Church, according to the Spirit of the Ecumenical Councils*], (Thessaloniki, 1971), pp. 37–38.

33 *P*, p. 63f. *O*, p. 399.

34 *O*, p. 426. According to Neophytos: "The Church of Christ confesses one baptism: not only in that she does not baptize anyone twice, but also that she baptizes everyone with one and the same baptism, and not some with

Chapter II: Interpretation of the Canon

d) Heretics of every kind as defined by St. Basil (Canon I), whom our theologians follow in this point also,[35] are outside the Church, and consequently their "baptism" is wholly without substance, i.e. "pseudo-baptism" and "not true,"[36] since it is performed outside the Church.[37] Hence, even in the event that it is performed by three immersions, i.e. in accordance with the correct form of the Church's baptism, it can in no way be considered "illumination," being as it is in essence "pollution."[38] Heretics cannot possibly have baptism, for they are unsound as regards the faith,[39] and thus "the baptism which they administer is of no benefit to them, since it lacks the correct faith."[40] According to Neophytos, the faith of the heretics "is anathematized, whereas ours is blessed. Nor is our baptism and theirs one and the same."[41] Therefore, as St. Nikodemos observes, even if the invocation of the Holy Trinity and the baptismal rite are done correctly by heretics, "those super-divine names

---

one kind of baptism and others with another" *E*, p. 142.

35 See *E*, p. 126; *P*, p. 587; *O*, pp. 89, 420.

36 *E*, p. 134; *P*, pp. 51, 55, 370; *O*, p. 413.

37 Cf. J. Kotsonis, *Περὶ τοῦ κύρους τῆς Ἱερωσύνης τῶν Ἀγγλικανῶν ἀπὸ τῆς ἀπόψεως τοῦ Κανονικοῦ Δικαίου τῆς Ὀρθοδόξου Ἐκκλησίας* [*On the Validity of Anglican Orders as seen from the Canon Law of the Orthodox Church*], (Athens, 1957), p. 18. According to Neophytos (*E*, p. 127): "the [baptism] belonging to heretics is completely rejected, while that of those in schism" is accepted, "when consecrated by the simple anointing with chrism," on the basis of Apostolic Canons XLVII and LXVIII, Canon I of Cyprian, and XLVII of Basil the Great.

38 *E*, pp. 133, 147f. Neophytos here invokes the holy Fathers Cyprian, Athanasios the Great, Basil the Great, Canon VIII of Laodicea and the Apostolic Canons.

39 *E*, pp. 142; 135–136.

40 *P*, pp. 52–53.

41 *E*, p. 137.

remain inactive and ineffective when pronounced by the mouths of heretics."[42]

Moreover, heretics cannot possibly have baptism, for they do not have priesthood. Priesthood and baptism are bound together,[43] and "it is wholly necessary to accept either both or neither."[44] Heretical baptism "is not capable of providing remission of sins,"[45] and therefore all heretics coming over to the Church must necessarily be baptized.[46] It is clear that these views are founded on St. Cyprian's Canon and Canon XLVII of St. Basil,[47] which, according to the *Kollyvades*, marked the way of *acrivia*,[48] according to which there is no room for discussion concerning, validity of heretical sacraments in themselves.[49]

---

42 *P*, p. 56. And according to Neophytos, "nor is simply trine immersion with the invocations in itself sufficient for the success of the sacrament," *E*, p. 147 xiv. This is so because "the true baptism of Apostolic Canon XLVII should not be thought of as being simply that which is performed in the Father and the Son and the Holy Spirit and in three immersions, but also that which is performed with a sound confession of the Trinity..." *E*, p. 139.

43 "It is the same principle for both baptism and ordination," *E*, p. 147 xxii. Cf. *O*, pp. 459, 492; *E*, p. 133f: "Heretics are neither Orthodox nor priests." *E*, p. 137. Cf. Apostolic Canon LXVIII, and *Apostolic Injunctions* VI, 15.

44 *E*, p 147 xxii. According to Apostolic Canon LXVIII, heretics do not have priesthood, and consequently "the rites performed by them are profane and destitute of grace and sanctification," *P*, pp. 50, 52. "According to the Apostolic Canon, their priests are false; hence, their baptism is surely also false," *E*, p 147 xiii.

45 *E*, p. 147 xiv. Correctly Neophytos adds: "For it does provide it, then they join the Church for no reason, and the heretics who do not join hear this."

46 *P*, p. 370.

47 See *E*, p. 132.

48 This was "ratified" by Canon II of Penthekte. *O*, p. 491. For how our writers understand "*acrivia*" and "*economia*," see pp. 57–65 of this study.

49 Ed. For more on the teachings of the Orthodox saints and Fathers in the East and Pre-Schism West on sacraments performed outside of the unity of the one Church, see An Orthodox Ethos Publication, *On the Reception of the Heterodox into the Orthodox Church: The Patristic Consensus and Criteria*, (Florence, AZ: Uncut Mountain Press, 2023), pp. 121–190.

Chapter II: Interpretation of the Canon

e) The altering of the "God-given" form of the Church's one baptism, "without urgent necessity,"[50] constitutes "an uncondonable breach of Apostolic tradition,"[51] and "an odious and abominable act."[52] According to Neophytos, baptism is "homologous to the dogmas,"[53] and "trine immersion" is itself also a "dogma."[54] Baptism is not a mere "ecclesiastical usage" that can be "considered on the basis of custom and tradition, but belongs to the faith itself."[55] Hence, to distinguish the confession from the form of the baptism is not allowable. To the question, "which is more important and essential, the external mode, or the faith?" Oikonomos responds: "both."[56] And he quotes St. Basil, according to whom "faith and baptism are two modes that are mutually inherent and undivided; for faith is perfected through baptism, while baptism is founded through faith."[57] The correct confession on faith must be accompanied by "perfect" baptism, for only this baptism "in return perfects the faith," according to Oikonomos.[58]

f) That trine immersion is requisite for the foundation of the sacrament befits its dogmatic nature. By the trine immersion, "we confess the dogma of the divinely sovereign

---

50 *O*, p. 398.

51 *Ibid.*

52 *O*, p. 485.

53 *E*, p. 147 xiv. Also according to Oikonomos, the "innovation" regarding the form of baptism "is not a heresy, i.e. not a dogmatic one according to the exact meaning of the word...It is, however, an adominable and execrable practice, not at all purifying any guilt of heresy whatsoever. It is the unholy invention of heretical men, and a falsification of the delivered form..." *O*, p. 485. In other words, it is the fruit of heresy!

54 *E*, p. 147 xvii. Cf. St. Basil's Canon I, and *On the Holy Spirit* 27, *PG* 32:185Cf.

55 *E*, p. 147 xiv.

56 *O*, p. 425.

57 *On the Holy Spirit* 12, *PG* 32:117B. Cf. *E*, p. 147 xiv, 147 xvii.

58 *O*, p. 426.

Trinity pronounced in the invocations"; and not only this, but also "the dogma of the dispensation of Christ our God and Savior," inasmuch as the three immersions and emersions "symbolically typify His death and burial, and His resurrection on the third day."[59] According to St. Nikodemos, it is not a matter of mere symbolism, but of reality, for "the person effects the Lord's death in himself. That is, the person who is baptized dies and is buried with Christ in the baptismal water" (cf. Rom. 6:9). Without the three immersions, it is "impossible for there to be in us the likeness of Christ's death and three-day burial." Yet, the Orthodox baptism at the same time typifies "the descent into Hades of the Lord's soul." Hence, "through the typification of Christ's burial," the body of the baptized person is fashioned by God; whereas "through the typification of the descent into Hades," his soul is deified. In this manner St. Nikodemos sums up the relevant patristic teaching.[60,61]

These presuppositions aid us in correctly assessing the theological standpoint of the *Kollyvades*, and of C. Oikonomos who was of one mind with them, regarding Canon VII of the Second Ecumenical Council, and in general the manner of receiving both earlier and later heretics.

2. Authenticity of the Canon

In the seventeenth century, the English canonist G. Beveridge (Beveregius) raised the question of the authenticity

---

59   *O*, p. 398–399. *M*, p. 266. Cf. Ware, p. 91ff.

60   *P*, p. 63f.

61   Ed. On the necessity of performing baptism in three full immersions in the name of the Holy Trinity according to Apostolic Canon 50 and the teachings of the saints and Holy Fathers, see also An Orthodox Ethos Publication, *On the Reception of the Heterodox into the Orthodox Church: The Patristic Consensus and Criteria*, (Florence, AZ: Uncut Mountain Press, 2023), pp. 45–56.

Chapter II: Interpretation of the Canon

of Canon VII of The Second Ecumenical Council,[62] when he demonstrated that it does not belong to the work of the Council because of its being a text of the fifth century.[63] Of course, for the Orthodox Church, the proving of this Canon's inauthenticity[64] in no way diminishes its authority (which was never disputed on Orthodox soil), inasmuch as its contents were repeated verbatim by Canon XCV of Penthekte, and hence it acquired Ecumenical and eternal authority.[65]

Only one of our theologians,[66] namely Neophytos Kafsokalyvitis, deals with the issue of the Canon's authenticity. He rejects it, something rather bold for the Greek-speaking world of the eighteenth century.[67] His argument, which fills

---

62 «ΣΥΝΟΔΙΚΟΝ», sive *Pandectae Canonum SS. Apostolorum et Conciliorum ab Ecclesia Graeca receptorum, nec non canonicarum SS. Patrum epistolarum; una cum scholiis antiquorum, singulis eorum annexis, et scriptis aliis huc spectantibus; quorum plurima e bibliothecae Bodleianae aliarumque MSS. Codicibus nunc primum edita; reliqua cum Iisdem MSS. Summa fide et diligentia collata. Totum opus in duos tomos divisum, Guilielmus Beveregius* Ecclesiae Anglicanae presbyter, recensuit, Prolegomenis munivit et annotationibus auxit, Oxonii, e theatro Sheldoniano, sumptibus Guilielmi Wells et Roberti Scott bibliop. Lond. MDCLXXII. See vol. II, p. 98ff. Cf. Mansi 3 :563/4, n. 2. Karl Joseph Hefele, *Conciliengeschichte*, 2nd ed. (Freiburg i. Br. 1856), pp. 12ff, 27.

63 The authenticity of only the first four Canons of the Council was defended. See A. P. Christophilopoulos, Ἑλληνικὸν Ἐκκλησιαστικὸν Δίκαιον [*Greek Ecclesiastical Law*] (Athens, 1965), p. 40. Cf. Karmiris, vol. I, p. 129 n.2. D. Georgiadis, «Τὸ βάπτισμα τῶν αἱρετικῶν» ("The baptism of heretics"), *Νέα Σιών* ΙΘ' (1924), p. 104. Ware, p. 72.

64 Of course, the opposite opinion also exists. The authenticity of Canon was defended by, among others, Chrysostomos Papadopoulos in his study: «Περὶ τοῦ βαπτίσματος τῶν ἑτεροδόξων» ["On the baptism of the non-Orthodox"], *Ἐκκλησιαστικὸς Φάρος* 14 (1915), p. 474.

65 See Karmiris. See Ware, p. 72 n. 1.

66 St Nikodemos does not deal with this problem. See e.g. *P*, pp. 154, 423, 590 et al.

67 He devotes a special chapter of his *Epitome* to the problem, titled: "On Canon VII of the Second Ecumenical Council and XCV of the Sixth" (pp. 147 xx–147 xxv).

many pages of his unpublished work, is based on the Western sources of his time.[68] It encompasses not only Canon VII of the Second Ecumenical Council, but also Canon XCV of Penthekte, which is "consonant with and the equivalent of Canon VII of the Second Council."[69] Neophytos considers both to be "not from a Council," but "from the epistle" to Martyrios of Antioch,[70] and consequently "interpolated,"[71] and clearly in opposition to the Apostolic Canons and those of St. Basil which were ratified by Penthekte.[72] Neophytos does not determine precisely when the interpolation of these Canons into the work of the two Ecumenical Councils occurred.[73] However, according to him, it is not certain that Penthekte did it.[74] In any event, it must have occurred before Photios and the monk Arsenios, who list both of the above-mentioned Canons together with the rest of the Canons of these Councils.[75] But this again does not substantiate their authenticity, for there exists evidence of the opposite in

---

68 He repeatedly quotes verbatim from the *Jus Graecoromanum* IV, pp. 290–291, and from the *ΣΥΝΟΔΙΚΟΝ* or *Pandectae* (of Beveridge). *E*, pp. 147 xx, 147 xxi, 147 xxii (quotes from vol. II, pp. 100, 501, 717, 748). Neophytos' argument, which he obviously took from Beveridge's work, is that the Canon is not found in the early translations (Latin, Arabic), nor in the Summaries of John the Scholastic and Symeon Magistros.

69 *E*, p. 147 xx.

70 Neophytos quotes the whole epistle (*E*, p. 147 xxiii-xiv), citing the *Jus Graecoromanum* IV, pp. 290–291, and the *Pandectae*, vol II, p. 100 (*E*, p. 147 xx-xxi).

71 *E*, pp. 147 xxi, 147 xxii.

72 *E*, p. 147 xx.

73 *E*, p. 147 xxi.

74 "Where is the indisputable proof that it [i.e. the 'custom' of Constantinople] was canonized by the Sixth Council?" *E*, p. 147 xxiii. Since the Canon is "verbatim," it belongs neither to the Second nor to the Sixth. (*E*, p. 147 xxiv).

75 Photios, *Nomokanon*, titl. iv, ch. xiv. Arsenios Monk, *Kanoniki Synopsis*, ch. xxxv and cxxxiv. *E*, p. 147 xx and 147 xxv.

Chapter II: Interpretation of the Canon

earlier writers who, by virtue of their antiquity, posses greater credibility.[76] So, Neophytos judges that Canon VII of the Second Council (together with Canon XCV of Penthekte) should be rejected, especially in order to escape the charges against the Orthodox Church by the "Lutherocalvinists."[77]

According to Neophytos, acceptance of the inauthenticity of these two Canons with good reason also weakens their authority, which otherwise constitutes a real cross for the Athonite monk who accepts the absoluteness and immovableness of the Cyprianic principle, according to which heretical baptism is without substance, never and nowise capable of being accepted by the Orthodox Church. Yet a reasonable explanation needed to be given for the evidence of the origin of the present Canon, as well as for the reason it was listed among the Canons of the Second Ecumenical Council. In this respect, Neophytos develops the following argument:

The "ownerless"[78] epistle of the Church of Constantinople to Martyrios of Antioch which contains Canon VII of the Second Ecumenical Council exactly, "which one parenthesis,"[79] does not refer to the Church's generally prevailing procedure, but rather "cites the Constantinopolitan custom." It is, consequently, of a local and

---

[76] "And yet, these Canons are not to be entered as indisputably authentic on the grounds of this minuscule evidence alone, for they are unknown to John and Symeon who were prior to Arsenios and Photios…Hence, John might be more trustworthy being earlier than Alexios, Arsenios and Photios… for he was nearer to the Second Council than they" *E*, p. 147 xx.

[77] "Hence, I think it is much better to reject Canon VII, and also Canon XCV of the Sixth Council, as having been interpolated, rather than, by reckoning them with the authentic Canons, have things that cannot be tolerated by my own conscience which is unable to reconcile what is unreconcilable, but most of all by the Lutherocalvinists who attack the catholic Church that she supposedly contradicts herself." *E*, p. 147 xx.

[78] For the writer is anonymous. *E*, pp 147 xx, 147 xxiii et al.

[79] *E*, p. 147 xxi.

not catholic, Ecumenical character. Besides—as he logically observes—had such a rule for the reception of converting heretics been imposed by virtue of Canon VII of the Second Ecumenical Council and hence been in usage by the Church at large, it would have been known to him who posed the question, and hence he would not have needed to seek the opinion of the Patriarch of Constantinople.[80] Therefore, that which is described in the epistle is just a "custom" of the Constantinopolitan Church which cannot assume catholic force and an obligatory character;[81] for "the city's prestige" cannot impose a mere local practice on the entire Church. He does accept that this practice had in fact prevailed in Constantinople from the time of the Arian controversy (4th cen.), due to the problem of the returning "converts to Arianism"[82] (i.e. baptized Orthodox Christians who converted to Arianism and then returned to Orthodoxy), whom the Church rightly did not rebaptize, but only chrismated. With the passage of time, however, the distinction between "Arians and converts to Arianism" became obscure. Hence the procedure followed in the case of the latter was applied also to the Arians, according to Neophytos, uncanonically.[83]

This explains why, on the one hand, this practice is "partly at variance with the Canons," and on the other hand, "contradicts itself."[84] The first arises from this Canon's opposition to Canon II of Penthekte, which

---

80 *Ibid.*

81 *E*, p. 147 xxi–xxii. He adds rather sharply: "The epistle seems to demand that everyone everywhere ought to follow whatever and however Constantinople practices!" *E*, p. 147 xxiii. The Constantinopolitans give "the orders of the synodal Canons second place after whatsoever custom of their own" (*ibid*). And he concludes: "How mighty is custom, and how hard to fight against!"

82 *E*, p. 147 xxiv.

83 *E*, p. 147 xxiv–xxv.

84 *E*, p. 147 xxi.

Chapter II: Interpretation of the Canon

"nowhere appears reversely to repeat anything it ratified."[85] The second materializes from the fact that the Canon accepts "the baptism of the Arians and Macedonians, but not their ordination," contrary to Apostolic Canon XLVII, also ratified by Penthekte.[86] It follows, therefore, that there is no justification for the claim that "the Sixth Council subsequently canonized the hitherto uncanonized prevailing Constantinopolitan practice concerning heretics," for in such a case the Council would have been contradicting itself.[87]

Since it was impossible to harmonize this Canon with the Apostolic Canons, Neophytos goes one step further and disputes the authority of this epistle, and thus even further weakens the creditability of the two above-mentioned Canons deriving therefrom. Thus, he considers that the epistle was written not by Patriarch Gennadios I (458–471), as it is accepted, but by Akakios (471–479), "of the heresy of the Acephaloi."[88] Basing his argument on the phrase in the epistle, "...of which (i.e. the catholic Church) Your Beatitude is the president and head," Neophytos remarks: "It [the epistle] can in no way be patriarchal, for it calls the bishop of Antioch the head of the catholic Church of Christ," something which is "improper and impious," for there is but one head of the Church, Christ![89]

---

85 *E*, pp. 140–141.

86 *E*, p. 147 xxii: "It both accepts and does not accept the heretics' ordination, and this a contradiction."

87 *E*, pp. 147 xxii–147 xxiii.

88 *E*, p. 147 xxi: "At any rate, one might consider the aforesaid epistle as belonging to Akakios who came after Anatolios, for it does not mention the Acephaloi-Severians together with those whom it requires to be chrismated!"

89 *E*, p. 147 xxi: "For it does not befit a Patriarch, and indeed of Constantinople, to call the bishop of Antioch the head of the catholic Church of Christ." *Ibid.*

In light of the above, Neophytos' conclusion is easily understood. The two Canons in question cannot be considered synodal,[90] but "spurious and false."[91] Then, rejoicing that he was able to remove the scandalous contradiction of Penthekte, he exclaims: "And glory to our holy God worshipped in Trinity, who showed to disciples what evaded the wise and teachers."[92] Thus, the manner of receiving heretics must be defined on the basis of the following Canons especially written for this: XLVII and LXVIII Apostolic; VIII and XIX of the First Ecumenical Council; VII and VIII of Laodicea; I of Carchedon-Carthage; and I and XLVII of St. Basil; all of which posses the required Ecumenical authority, for "they were ratified" by Canons I of the Fourth, II of Penthekte, and I and XI of the Seventh Ecumenical Councils.[93]

Be that as it may, Neophytos closes his critique on the authenticity of Canon VII of the Second Ecumenical Council with a statement, obviously added later, which shows, among other things, his sincerity and objectivity. He writes that, "sufficient time having elapsed since the matters pertaining to the aforementioned two Canons were examined from the compendiums of Canons," he noticed in the fourth act of the Seventh Ecumenical Council that the Fathers of that Council read Canon LXXXII (should read CII) of the Sixth (Penthekte) Council from the original Acts of the Council. In the sixth act it expressly says that the Sixth Ecumenical Council "issued Canons…reaching in number one hundred and two," which also agrees with the testimony of Photios. Thus, Neophytos is forced to admit:

---

90   *E*, p. 147 xxiv.
91   *E*, p. 147 xxii.
92   *E*, p. 147 xxiii.
93   *Ibid.*

Chapter II: Interpretation of the Canon

"Hence, the things pertaining to Canon VII of the Second Ecumenical Council, which we heretofore conjecturally examined from the ancient [compendiums], now indeed appear to be obviously repudiated on the grounds of Canon XCV of the Sixth Council." Yet, he again ascertains that the contradiction, according to him, of Penthekte is not resolved. For, since the Seventh Ecumenical Council endorses Canon XCV of Penthekte, "it remains for someone to examine and devise another solution as regards this Canon's apparent partial disaccord with both the Apostolic Canons and Canon I of St. Basil which the Sixth and Seventh Councils ratified."[94] The above contradiction continues to hold, for the Arians are, on the basis of the Apostolic Canons and according to St. Basil, considered as being in need of baptism, while by Canon XCV of Penthekte as needing chrismation only, even though according to the Seventh Council (act vi, tome ii) they are not merely heretics, but "the same as pagans."

Neophytos does not continue. He cannot continue! The question remains for him unsolved. Of course, this is easy to explain, for Neophytos did not tolerate the exercise of *economia* towards heretics. As will appear below, the principle of *economia* removes what Neophytos considers a contradiction, and demonstrates the unity of the holy Canons of the Orthodox Church.

Of course, in confronting those whose position regarding the manner of receiving later heretics was based upon these two Canons, Neophytos, loyal to his Church's tradition, does use Canon VII of the Second Ecumenical Council,[95] putting aside the problem of its authenticity. In most cases, however, he uses it in conjunction with Canon XCV of Penthekte,

---

94   *E*, p. 147 xxv.
95   See e.g. *E*, pp. 127, 131, 132, 139f.

and indeed in the form: "the Sixth Council together with the Second,"[96] or "the Second and Sixth."[97] This shows that the authenticity of Canon VII of the Second Ecumenical Council depended on Canon XCV of Penthekte, and that without a doubt it remained diminished in his conscience because of the lack of authenticity, and also because of the problems it created, as we shall see further on.

3. Interpretation of the Canon

According to our writers, Canon VII of the Second Ecumenical Council provides an immediate solution to the question, "How should heretics who come over to Orthodoxy be received?"[98] The canonical frame of reference within which this Canon can be correctly interpreted is established by the following Canons: XLVI, XLVII, L, and LXVIII Apostolic; I of Carchedon-Carthage (3rd cen.); VII and VIII of Laodicea; VIII and XIX of the First Ecumenical Council; I, V, XX, and XLVII of St. Basil; XCV of Penthekte; and LVII and LXXX of Carthage (5th cen.).[99] Moreover, this Canon should be examined in conjunction with Canon XCV of Penthekte, which "is nothing else but a reiteration of it."[100]

This Canon, however, presents many difficulties in its interpretation. For, taken literally, it is clearly contrary to the practice of the Church canonically formulated through St. Cyprian and other Fathers (e.g. St. Basil).[101] And, as we

---

96 E.g. *E*, p. 132.
97 E.g. *E*, p. 139.
98 *O*, p. 419. Cf. *P*, p. 92.
99 *P*, p. 165 et al. *E*, throughout *O*, pp. 419–420, 453–454. For the texts of these Canons, see Appendix I below.
100 *E*, p. 147 xx; *P*, p. 165; *O*, pp. 419–420.
101 Cf. Christophilopoulos, p. 119; *E*, pp. 129f, 135f; and *P*, p. 370.

Chapter II: Interpretation of the Canon

have seen, our theologians accept that practice as deriving from the early Church and as being in agreement with the Apostolic Canons, and therefore as the only canonical and inviolable practice. Thus, with good reason St. Nikodemos poses the question: Why did the Second Ecumenical Council "not reject the baptism of all heretics, in accordance with the Apostolic Canons and the Council presided over by St. Cyprian, and all the rest of the great and God-bearing Fathers..., but accepted the baptism of some heretics while not that of others?"[102] The classification of heretics into those who are in need of baptism and those who are not is the core of the problem created by this Canon. To begin with, this classifying is considered by our writers "completely reprobate," on the basis of the Canons of St. Cyprian and St. Basil. It has already been said above that according to them, heretics of any kind are outside the Church and do not even have baptism, and therefore without any exception are in need of baptism.[103] The problem becomes even more acute, for the Second Ecumenical Council appeared tolerant and accommodating towards the "more impious" among the heretics of that time, namely the Arians and Macedonians, "who reject the divinity of our Lord Jesus Christ," and "who blaspheme against the Holy Spirit."[104] Thus at first sight, there seems to be disagreement between the holy Councils and the patristic Canons, for two Ecumenical Councils (the Second by its Canon VII, and Penthekte by its Canon XCV) come into conflict not only with the above-mentioned Fathers, but also with the Apostolic Canons (e.g. XLVI), which Penthekte—and through it the catholic Church—ratified notwithstanding, and which, according to

---

102 *P*, p. 53.
103 *P*, p. 55.
104 *O*, p. 420.

St. Nikodemos, "command the opposite."¹⁰⁵ This, then, is the problem created by these Canons.

In the effort to remove this disaccord, some canonists have held the view that Ecumenical Councils may review or rescind the canonical decisions of the Fathers, for "it is unheard of that one [Father] be preferred over an Ecumenical or Local Council."¹⁰⁶ The ratification of the Canons of the holy Fathers by Ecumenical Councils does not, according to this view, also indicate the affirmation of any contradiction that might consequently arise; for, quite simply, the Councils prevail, according to the well-known principle: "the inferior is blessed by the superior" (Heb. 7:7). Thus the Councils prevail, in a way setting in disuse the Canons formulated prior to them. Moreover, even Zonaras himself, in confronting the "antitheis" of Canon VII of the Second Ecumenical Council and the Canon of Carchedon-Carthage, which is essentially the Canon of St. Cyprian, writes: "In this chapter, the two Councils introduce opposites. The decisions of the Second Council prevail, because it is later and because it is Ecumenical; moreover, thereat together present were the patriarchs themselves or their vicars from all the patriarchal sees."¹⁰⁷

Our theologians, however, living the Church's tradition and knowing from immediate experience the place of the holy Fathers in her life, are not satisfied with this answer. They do not admit even the slightest discrepancy between Fathers and Councils.¹⁰⁸ The authority of the holy Fathers

---

105 *P*, p. 55.

106 *E*, p. 144.

107 *PG* 137:1103.

108 *E*, p. 144: "In fact, Basil the Great and Athanasios and Cyprian and his synod were not given precedence, but rather equal standing with the Sixth and Seventh Ecumenical Councils which were in agreement with each one of them." Cf. *O*, p. 488. St. Nikodemos also notes: "there is no

Chapter II: Interpretation of the Canon 55

is panegyrically accepted by all of our writers. But of greater interest is the extensive analysis on this point too by Neophytos Kafsokalyvitis.[109]

According to Neophytos, the Councils—and in this case the Second and Penthekte Ecumenical Councils—do not annul the holy Fathers, whose authority is especially apparent in these very (Ecumenical) Councils, "the theology and decisions of which cannot be understood without the theological input of the Fathers and Doctors."[110] He offers characteristic examples: The divine Chrysostom "was given precedence" over the Council of Neocaesaria in Canon XVI of Penthekte, and Gregory the Theologian in Canon LXIV of the same Council. "Likewise, the Seventh Council, having cited Basil the Great as witness of what it defined in Canons XVI, XIX, and XX, admittedly gave him precedence over itself..."[111] St. Basil's authority especially is recognized at all "the Ecumenical Councils after him."[112] Neophytos thus concludes: "We say that the Ecumenical doctors have precedence over Ecumenical Councils not so as to refute what these Councils bade—God forbid, for they sided with the Councils—but rather to show how much they were revered by the Councils. ...Indeed the Ecumenical Councils rely on the holy and wise Fathers."[113]

Neophytos' conclusion is that the Second Ecumenical Council in no way ignored or set aside the holy Fathers prior to it (Cyprian, Athanasios, Basil, Gregory the Theologian, etc.), "who call heretical baptism a pollution," and who

---

contradiction or opposition between them" *P*, p. 54.

109 *E*, p. 144ff.

110 S. G. Papadopoulos, *Patrologia*, vol. I (Athens, 1977), p. 68.

111 *E*, p. 144.

112 *Ibid.* The Seventh Ecumenical Council calls Basil the Great a "Father" thereof. Cf. Canon XX of Penthekte also.

113 *E*, p. 145.

particularly reject Arian baptism as being "reprobate."[114] This is even more so true with Penthekte, which cannot at the same time "ratify" and rescind the Canon of Carchedon-Carthage and thus contradict itself. For although "the Second Council in its Canon VII passed over [the Canon of Carchedon-Carthage] and limited it to the locality where it was in force, yet the Sixth Council in its Canon II ratified it, and thus admittedly rendered it Ecumenical."[115] So, if Canons VII of the Second Ecumenical and XCV of the Penthekte appear to attach a local character to the Canon of Cyprian's Council, in any event Canon II of Penthekte gave it Ecumenical authority. For, "local and particular [Canons], when ratified by the catholic [Church], also became catholic."[116] No distinction of importance among the sacred Canons of the Church is allowed.[117]

Since, then, it is impossible for an Ecumenical Council to annul itself, there remains for Neophytos the justified question: "I cease not to inquire," he says, "for what reason the Sixth Council (and consequently also the Second) ever accepted the inefficacious and totally unacceptable and, according to Apostolic Canon XLVI, rejected rites of those who for heresy were both synodically unfrocked and publicly banished from the Church and anathematized (i.e. Arians and Macedonians)."[118] He continues: "Moreover, I am still puzzled, and I think that so are all canonists. Let him who in the Lord is able to do so resolve the question and demonstrate the agreement of the Ecumenical Councils with the Apostolic Canons and those of St. Basil that they

---

114 *Ibid.*
115 *E*, p. 147 i.
116 *E*, p. 147 ii.
117 *P*, p. 52, 119.
118 *E*, p. 147 xii.

ratified..."[119] There must be, therefore, another explanation regarding the manner of action of these two Ecumenical Councils, in spite of the fact that especially Penthekte "ratifies" Canons which otherwise it appears to "annul."[120]

Our theologians do not leave the question unsolved. Although their answers preserve the individual character of each and thus differ on secondary points, yet they reach the same conclusions in consequence of their oneness of mind.

The position of the Second Ecumenical Council towards the Arians and Macedonians can be explained, according to St. Nikodemos, if we take into consideration that the Church "has two modes of governing and correcting," namely, *acrivia* = precision or rigorism[121], and *economia* = concession or dispensation. Whereas "the Apostles" and the earlier Councils and Fathers applied *acrivia*,[122] the two Ecumenical Councils accepted *economia*.[123] So, this alternation of *acrivia* and *economia* under certain defined conditions removes any hint of contradiction among the holy Canons and the Councils.[124] According to this saint, the Second Ecumenical

---

119 *E*, p. 147 xiv.

120 *P*, p. 54. *E*, pp. 140, 147 xi.

121 Ed. Or "exactitude."

122 *P*, pp. 368, 587f. Cf. Canon I of Carchedon-Carthage ("we pronounce no recent opinion or one that has only now been established, but on the contrary...that which of old was tested with all precision [Gk. *acrivia*] and care by our predecessors"); and Canon I of St. Basil ("it is not our responsibility to return them a favor, but to serve the precision [Gk. *acrivia*] of the Canons").

123 *P*, p. 53.

124 Ed. Some modern authors have claimed that the *acrivia/economia* interpretive key for seeming contradictions in the canons regarding the reception of heretics was a new teaching developed by St. Nikodemos and the Kollyvades Fathers in the 18th century. In fact, the distinction between *acrivia* and *economia* is found in St. Basil's Canons 1 and 47 that were adopted by the Ecumenical Councils. Before the Kollyvades Fathers, the ancient canonists, including Monk John Zonaras in the 12th century

Council "kept the Canon partially,"[125] acting "in accordance with *economia* and concession."[126] *Economia*, being a fruit of the Church's pastoral and remedial ministry, was exercised for provisional-historical reasons. The heretics in question were many in number and politically strong.[127] Hence the synodal Fathers showed leniency, "in order to attract them to Orthodoxy and to correct them more easily," and "so that it might not happen that they further infuriate them against the Church and the Christians, and the evil thus become worse."[128] The exercise of *economia*, therefore, was not arbitrary, but justified, having in view the salvation of the heretics and the peace of the Church.

According to Neophytos, himself unable to deviate from Cyprian's principle regarding the invalidity of heretical sacraments, "this *economia* in general…which even prior to the Second Council was prevalent in lieu of a Canon, accepted the rites of the Arians just as it did those of the schismatics, as one can surmise from the Second Council."[129] However, there was, according to him, an important reason which made *economia* not only possible, but also necessary. Both the Sixth and the Second Ecumenical Councils speak about "those heretics who originally came from us."[130] That is, when

---

and Hieromonk Matthew Blastares in the 14th century, also understood that canons allowing for some heretics to be received by a manner other than baptism was by exception or *economia*. For more examples of the understanding of *economia* and *acrivia* prior to the 18th century, see An Orthodox Ethos Publication, *On the Reception of the Heterodox into the Orthodox Church: The Patristic Consensus and Criteria*, (Florence, AZ: Uncut Mountain Press, 2023), pp. 193–199.

125 *P*, p. 370.
126 *P*, p. 53.
127 *Ibid.*
128 *Ibid.*
129 *E*, p. 147 xi.
130 *E*, p. 131.

Chapter II: Interpretation of the Canon 59

those of the Orthodox who had become Arians returned again, they were not baptized.[131] On the other hand, "those who had become Arians, but who had not previously been Orthodox, and who had not previously undergone Orthodox baptism, but only that of the heretics," would need to be baptized as being unbaptized.[132] But "most of them (Arians and Macedonians) who originally came from the Orthodox were intermingled [with those who were originally Arians], and without admitting the truth attached themselves to the [Orthodox] clergy," according to Epiphanios;[133] hence (also according to St. Basil),[134] "because of the confusion there can be no distinction between Orthodox and heretics." Therefore the Council was forced to exercise *economia*,[135] which according to Neophytos can only be exercised in the case of schismatics.[136]

St. Nikodemos defends a position parallel to this one. Interpreting St. Cyprian's Canon, he comments: "But if one searches well, he will find that most of those heretics whom the Second Ecumenical Council received by *economia* were from among the baptized clergy who had fallen into heresy, and this is why the Council used this *economia*."[137] What is common to both these views is the conviction that those who were received "by *economia*" preserved the "Church's baptism," i.e. the three immersions and emersions. According to Neophytos, on account of the Arians this

---

131 *E*, p. 147 xxiv. Cf. *E*, p. 147 iv.
132 *E*, p. 147 v.
133 *Against heresies* III, 1, *PG* 42:448A.
134 *On the holy Spirit* 3, *PG* 32:76.
135 *E*, p. 127. Cf. *E*, p. 141. Cf. *O*, p. 475.
136 *E*, p. 131. "And in a word, the baptism belonging to heretics is to be completely rejected, while that of schismatics is to be accepted when it is consecrated by mere anointing with chrism." *E*, p. 127.
137 *P*, p. 370.

"custom" was prevalent in Constantinople. Hence it was included in the epistle "To Martyrios," and finally was canonized by Penthekte through its Canon XCV; for it had found its way into Councils—the Second Ecumenical and Penthekte—that, again, had met in the same city of Constantinople!

Oikonomos also accepts the early Councils' free exercise, from time to time, of both *acrivia* and *economia* without the slightest conflict among the holy Canons. According to him, the Apostolic Canons "were set for *acrivia*." The Second Ecumenical and Penthekte Councils, however, used *economia* for historical reasons ("the then times demanding it").[138]

The Second Ecumenical Council's classification of heretics into those in need of baptism and those in need of chrismation, however, was based, according to our writers, on a specific ecclesiological and canonical assumption. Heretics who were required to be baptized had, according to Oikonomos, as "a common characteristic…not only the utter blasphemy regarding the divine dogmas, but mostly the impious transgression as regards the kind of baptism they have." This transgression was "twofold": "regarding the invocation of the persons of the All-holy Trinity,"[139] and "regarding the trine immersion of the person baptized."[140]

Thus, the practice of baptizing converting heretics was "canonized" by Canon VII of the Second Ecumenical Council, not so much "on account of their erroneous beliefs regarding the divine dogma," for they renounced these by their conversion and through the mandatory written statement they submitted; "but first and foremost on account

---

138 *O*, pp. 488, 491. Cf. Ch. Androutsos, Δογματική τῆς Ὀρθοδόξου Ἀνατολικῆῆς Ἐκκλησίας [*Dogmatics of the Orthodox Eastern Church*] (Athens, 1956), p. 301f.

139 *O*, p. 421: "Such was the baptism of those who baptized into three unoriginates, or three sons, or three paracletes."

140 *O*, p. 421.

Chapter II: Interpretation of the Canon   61

of their baptismal rite, which is profane and inefficacious because it is wholly incorrect as regards the divine invocations and/or the three immersions."[141] Hence, adds St. Nikodemos, those belonging to this group (Eunomians, Montanists, Sabellians, "and all other heresies"[142]), were without any possible exception received "as pagans," i.e. as "wholly unbaptized." For "either they had never been baptized, or else they had been baptized, but not correctly and in the manner the Orthodox are baptized. Hence, they are not considered as having been baptized at all."[143] So, what is understood as "baptism" by these writers, as well as by the (early) Fathers of the Church, is not merely entrance into the Church, but enrolment into her according to a specific Apostolic manner, i.e. by three immersions.

The exercise of *economia* towards the Arians and Macedonians does not at all mean that the Council overlooked the "faith," but that the degree of their deviation from the Orthodox faith was not of primary importance for the Council.[144] *Economia* was possible, because these heretics "preserved the Apostolic tradition in their own baptism; for they baptized according to the Lord's command, in the name of the Father and of the Son and of the Holy Spirit, and with three immersions and emersions."[145] The correct

---

141 *O*, p. 423.

142 Ed. Canon 7 of the Second Ecumenical Council and Canon 95 of the Penthekte Ecumenical Council, though allowing certain specifically named heretics to be received by *economia*, stated that "all other heresies" were to be received by baptism, thereby showing baptism to be the standard means of receiving heretics. See An Orthodox Ethos Publication, *On the Reception of the Heterodox into the Orthodox Church: The Patristic Consensus and Criteria*, (Florence, AZ: Uncut Mountain Press, 2023), pp. 91–99.

143 *P*, pp. 164 and 55. Cf. *P*, p. 587f.; *M*, p. 263; *O*, p. 490 ("they had no baptism whatsoever, wherefore the Church prescribed to baptize them as well").

144 Cf. Kotsonis, (*On the validity…*), p. 26.

145 *O*, p. 422.

performance of the sacrament constituted the criterion for the admission of their baptism. Thus, "the impiety of their beliefs was remedied through their written statement" and "through divine chrismation," which was given "to certify their confession and faith,... so that they might become participants in Christ's kingdom and in the gift of the Spirit, of which they had been deprived." Some of them, in fact, had perhaps not even been anointed with chrism, as for example the Novatians, towards whom the Council of Laodicea exercised *economia*.[146] But towards the Eunomians, it was never possible for the Council to exercise *economia*, for they had received a "single-immersion baptism," i.e. one different from the Church's. An alteration of the form of the sacrament which destroys its unity, i.e. the correspondence of the external and internal element, was for the Council decisively significant. For *economia* too, according to Oikonomos who invokes the holy Fathers, has its limits: "*Economia* is permissible as long as it involves no violation of the law," said Chrysostom proverbially.[147] Canon VII of the Second Ecumenical Council, says Oikonomos, omitted reference to the Eunomian "blasphemy regarding the invocation,...for the sake of brevity"; the equally important imperfection in the form of the sacrament, i.e. the single immersion, was sufficient.[148]

Thus it is proven, according to Oikonomos, that "there is no contradiction in the Canons concerning baptism."[149] The interpretation of the holy Canons on the basis of the scheme *acrivia/economia* removes any seeming disharmony among them. It is worthy of notice, however, that these

---

146 *O*, pp. 422–423, 424, 488–489.
147 *O*, pp. 433, 434 (and n. 1). Cf. Evlogios of Alexandria, *PG* 103:953.
148 *O*, p. 421.
149 *O*, p. 488.

Chapter II: Interpretation of the Canon

theologians understand *economia* as leniency-concession in the face of the Church's precision, i.e. as a pastoral measure; while *acrivia* they understand as a theological measure which demands the loyal and precise adherence to the word of God that constitutes the Church's normal practice.[150] In this case, however, the Church's normal practice is not defined by the Ecumenical Councils, but by the "Apostolic" and "patristic" Canons,[151] which after their Ecumenical accreditation are nowise inferior in authority to synodal Canons, and indeed those of the Ecumenical Councils. In this particular case, the Ecumenical Councils, like the Second and Penthekte, without repudiating *acrivia*, provide a solution "by *economia*."[152] According to our writers, there is not only oneness of spirit among our Church's sacred Canons, but also they are of equal force and equal validity, inasmuch as her holy Canons are all "Ecumenical." Thus, the Canons of the Ecumenical Councils, and in this case of the Second and Penthekte, do not set the older Canons into disuse, nor abolish them.[153] Such a position is,

---

150 According to Ch. Androutsos, Συμβολικὴ ἐξ ἐπόψεως ὀρθοδόξου [*Symbology from an Orthodox Point of View*], 3rd ed. (Thessaloniki, 1963), pp. 303–304: *economia* is "a deviation from what is in principle correct and true." Cf. A. Alivizatos, Ἡ Οἰκονομία κατὰ τὸ Κανονικὸν Δίκαιον τῆς Ὀρθοδόξου Ἐκκλησίας [*Dispensation according to Canon Law of the Orthodox Church*], (Athens, 1949), p. 21. J. Kotsonis, Προβλήματα τῆς «Ἐκκλησιαστικῆς Οἰκονομίας» [*Problems in "Ecclesiastical Dispensation"*], (Athens, 1957), p. 207f. P. Boumis, Ἡ ἐκκλησιαστικὴ οἰκονομία κατὰ τὸ Κανονικὸν Δίκαιον [*Ecclesiastical Dispensation according to Canon Law*], (Athens, 1971), p. 7.

151 The practice to which Canon I of Carthedon-Carthage attests was applied throughout the entire fourth century, as this is shown from Canons XIX of the First Council, VIII of Laodicea, I and XLVII of St. Basil, and XLVI and LXVIII Apostolic.

152 Likewise, Canon XII of Penthekte applies a solution "by *economia*." See P. I. Boumis, Τὸ ἔγγαμον τῶν Ἐπισκόπων [*The Marriage of Bishops*] (Athens, 1981), p. 10.

153 Cf. the opinion of J. Kotsonis: "Wherever in previous Canons something is ordered contrary to this holy Canon (i.e. XCV of Penthekte), that which is

for these theologians, legalistic in the extreme and clearly anti-ecclesial, inasmuch as *acrivia* and *economia* can easily co-exist in the Church's canonical order. The possibility of using both *acrivia* and *economia* insures the Church's freedom and rules out her becoming confined to any legal forms whatsoever. But our writers would not be in agreement with the principle that *acrivia* is that which was decreed by the Ecumenical Councils, and *economia* is any divergence therefrom.[154] For them, *acrivia* is the practice of the Church emanating from her self-understanding, according to which, outside of her there are neither sacraments nor salvation.

Thus, the *economia* that was used by the Second Ecumenical Council on the basis, as we saw, of specific presuppositions, does not in any way eliminate the Church's *acrivia*. According to St. Nikodemos, "the *economia* that some Fathers temporarily used can neither be thought of as law nor taken as an example."[155] The context in which St. Nikodemos made this comment indicates that he had in mind the Fathers of the Second Ecumenical Council. Oikonomos states the identical position even more clearly, saying: The Ecumenical Councils "did not rescind the Canons legislated in *acrivia*; for some might wish to abide by them for the sake of the complete ease of their conscience, and in accordance with their prevailing ancient ethos." Neophytos supports the same position,[156] and in his usual

---

ordered by this Canon prevails." Article in *Θ.Η.Ε.*, vol. 2 (1963), col. 1093. Same author, *(Problems...)*, 187, n. 571. Cf. A. Christophilopoulos, «Ἡ εἰς τὴν Ὀρθοδοξίαν προσέλευσις...» ["The coming over to Orthodoxy..."], *Θεολογία* ΚΖ' (1956), p. 59.

154 See Kotsonis, *(Problems...)*, pp. 91-93. Same author, *(On the validity...)*, p. 27.

155 *P*, p. 371. That is why in his footnote to Canon XX of St. Basil (*P*, p. 605) he points out: "See how according to this Canon the Church does not receive heretics without baptizing them, even if Canon VII of the Second Ecumenical Council by *economia* receives certain heretics without baptism."

156 *O*, p. 488. Cf. *E*, p. 147 xi: "If the *acrivia* of the Canons receives by baptism

manner he formulates the following practical syllogism: "Only the Sixth together with the Second voted that to a certain extent heretics be chrismated." On the other hand, the holy Fathers (Cyprian, Basil, Athanasios, etc.), and the Local Council of Laodicea, and also the Apostolic Canons, decree "simply to baptize" them, as do also the Sixth and Seventh Ecumenical Councils, "which ratify what they had done." And according to Canon VI of the First Ecumenical Council, and Canon XIX of the Council of Antioch, "the vote of the majority rules." So he concludes: "Therefore, according to the majority vote, heretics are in need of baptism; or according to the minority, some are in need only of chrismation." It is ascertained, however, that one finds in the holy Canons "many more votes for baptism than for mere chrismation."[157] Perhaps one should not be quick simply to reject this "argument" of Neophytos', but rather should try to discern his ultimate aim. With this argument he wants to prove what was said above: namely, that the Second and Penthekte Councils used *economia* for specific, practical reasons only, and by exception.

So, our writers arrive together at the unanimous decision that, according to the Church's canonical practice, as a rule *acrivia* should be applied to heretics who convert to Orthodoxy; in other words, they should be baptized, since in any case, neither by *acrivia* nor by *economia* can heretical sacraments be considered valid.[158]

---

those whom custom chrismates, then he who rather follows *acrivia* on those who accept it would not err, for he will have done not contrary to custom, but more than the custom."

157 *E*, p. 132.
158 Kotsonis, *(Problems…)*, p. 201ff. St. Nikodemos typically comments: "Hence, if St. Basil rejects the baptismal rite of schismatics because they lacked the grace to accomplish sacraments, then it is superfluous even to ask if we should baptize heretics" (*P*, p. 52).

4. Summary

In this way, then, is Canon VII of the Second Ecumenical Council interpreted by the *Kollyvades* and C. Oikonomos. These writers are in agreement with the canonists before them, as far the understanding of the Canon in question is concerned. In conclusion, we can summarize their teaching and positions as follows:

a.) By the principle of *economia*, all seeming disaccord between this Canon and those previous Canons which are considered to be in disagreement with it is removed. There is no disaccord among the Church's holy Canons,[159] which in this seemingly curious antinomy retain their unity and preserve the freedom in Christ.

b.) The Second Ecumenical Council, in exercising *economia* towards certain *specifically named* heretics, did not leave the ground open for the inclusion in his category of any other heretics unchecked. *Economia* was used for important historical and pastoral reasons, without revoking the *acrivia* ratified by the second part of the Canon and exercised on other heretics, again not arbitrarily!

c.) The exercise of *economia* was possible, because there existed the *absolutely necessary* "formal" conditions, i.e. the correct execution of the sacrament by these heretics with three immersions and emersions.[160] The rejection of the single-immersion baptism of the Eunomians, who were classified among the wholly unbaptized, indicates the Council's—and consequently the catholic Church's—condemnation

---

159 See V. I. Pheides, Ἱστορικοκανονικαὶ καὶ ἐκκλησιολογικαὶ προϋποθέσεις ἑρμηνείας τῶν ἱερῶν κανόνων [*Historico-canonical and ecclesiological presuppositions for an interpretation of the Sacred Canons*], (Athens, 1972), p. 44.

160 Cf. Zonaras and Valsamon in: G. A. Rallis and M. Potlis, Σύνταγμα τῶν θείων καὶ ἱερῶν κανόνων [*Collection of the divine and sacred Canons*], vol. II (Athens, 1852), pp. 189, 191. Cf. Rinne, p. 38 (and n. 6).

of any alteration in the form of the sacrament of baptism, which alteration is sufficient to render the exercise of *economia* towards these heretics entirely impossible. In this case, according to Oikonomos: "The danger concerning all: they were not born of water and spirit, nor were they through baptism buried with Christ into His death."[161] That is to say, they are unbaptized, and therefore bereft of the regeneration in Christ.

The problem, in the final analysis, is not the disregard or rejection of a mere "form," but something much deeper: namely, disobedience to Christ's commandment ("...*baptizing them*..." Mt. 28:19), and unfaithfulness to the Church's tradition. And this tradition, if not held fast in its totality as *pleroma*-fullness of life, runs the risk of becoming estranged, and consequently of losing its local force!

---

161 *O*, p. 490. He clearly specifies what he means: "For either they did not obtain divine baptism, or if they did, it was not done correctly or according to the ritual of the Orthodox Church."

CHAPTER III
Application of the Canon

IT WAS previously stated at the beginning of this study that in the eighteenth century, Canon VII of the Second Ecumenical Council was interpreted in the context of a search for a solution to the problem concerning the reception of converts from the West (i.e. Europe), and especially Latins. There had already preceded a lengthy period of irresolution among the Orthodox over the issue.[162] Patriarch Cyril V's solution (1755) had not been accepted by all as the only prescribed and correct one.[163] The question posed by both sides was whether the Second Ecumenical Council's distinction of the heretics by *economia* could also be made in the case of the Latins. After all, this was the Canon (and also, of course, Canon XCV of Penthekte) on which those who had applied this solution in the past had relied. The difference we observe on this issue, however,

---

162 See Karmiris, vol. II, pp. 972ff, 979f; Metropolitan Germanos of Ainos, «Περὶ τοῦ κύρους τοῦ βαπτίσματος τῶν αἱρετικῶν» ["On the validity of heretical baptism"], *Ὀρθοδοξία* ΚΖ΄ (1952), p. 301ff.

163 It is sufficient to read the "censorious" texts "against the rebaptizers" of the eighteenth century that this issue gave rise to. See Skouvaras, pp. 94ff, 122ff; Cf. Metropolitan Germanos of Ainos, p. 314.

Chapter III: Application of the Canon 69

was heightened by the disagreement among the Orthodox over the classification of the Latins: as heretics, or as schismatics.[164] For obviously only those who considered Latins heretics were faced with the problem of applying Canon VII to them. Our writers belong to this group, and their relevant teaching we present below.

1. Latins are "heretics" and "unbaptized"

Possessing a profound knowledge of the Church's history after the schism and of the disagreement among the Orthodox regarding the characterization of the Latins as heretics or as schismatics, and also expressing their own theological self-awareness, our writers—in absolute agreement with one another and without the slightest doubt—consider the Latins (and by extension the Lutherocalvinists) to be heretics. The Latins "are heretics," asserts St. Nikodemos; and "we abominate them as heretics, i.e. like Arians or Sabellians or Pneumatomachoi-Macedonians."[165] The aim of the saint's direct reference to the early, major heretics is to show that the Latins are, as he says elsewhere, "age-old heretics,"[166] i.e. in the same sense as those that appeared in the early undivided Church. To support his claim, he invokes the testimonies of Patriarch Dositheos, Elias Meniates, St. Mark of Ephesus, and others.

Neophytos expresses himself in the same manner regarding the Latins. "The Latins differ from Orthodoxy on five points. As regards the other [four] differences, they are schismatics. Only as regards the Spirit's procession also from the Son are they heretics, together with the Lutherocalvinists

---

164 See, in this regard, the very comprehensive chapter: "Greeks and Latins: Hostility and Friendship," in Ware, p. 16ff.

165 *P*, pp. 55, 56.

166 *P*, p. 55.

who believe the same."[167] The heretical *filioque* dogma of the Latins[168] was sufficient for them to be considered heretics; for, of course, they had not yet dogmatized the papal doctrines on primacy and infallibility. To the commonly advanced objection that there was only one essential Latin dogmatic difference, Neophytos responds that the same holds true for the Latins as did once for the Iconoclasts: "Inasmuch as they differed not from us as regards faith in God, they were not heretics, but schismatics. But since, by rejecting the venerable icons they also rejected Christ who was thereon portrayed, they were worse than heretics themselves."[169] Similarly, the one difference of the Latins, "pertaining directly to the faith in God," is vital and decisive.[170] Besides, heresy, being potent in character, is not judged by the number of deviations from the truth; for, according to the evangelical saying: "Whoever fails in one point has become guilty of all" (cf. Jas. 2:10). Every heresy indicates a prior alteration of the Church's spiritual presuppositions, i.e. the mystico-niptic, patristic experience. This is the firm conviction of our writers as well.

The Latins are also considered heretics by Athanasios Parios[171] and C. Oikonomos, because of the *filioque* innovation. According to Oikonomos, the Latins, "being heretics and not merely schismatics,"[172] "heretically

---

167 *E*, p. 147 ix.

168 One may see the importance and the dimensions of the Latin *"filioque"* dogma in the studies by Prof. Fr. John Romanides, Δογματικὴ καὶ Συμβολικὴ Θεολογία τῆς Ὀρθοδόξου Καθολικῆς Ἐκκλησίας [*Dogmatic and Symbolic Theology of the Orthodox Catholic Church*], vol. 1 (Thessaloniki, 1973), pp. 289ff, 342ff, 379ff. "The Filioque," (Anglican-Orthodox Joint Doctrinal Discussions) (Athens, 1978).

169 *E*, p. 147 ix.

170 *E*, p. 127. "Just short of being pious…they are not pious at all." *E*, p. 147 viii.

171 *M*, pp. 263, 265.

172 *O*, p. 459.

innovate in other matters, and particularly as regards the divine Creed."¹⁷³ Hence he also speaks about the "papist heresy,"¹⁷⁴ thus intimating the contribution to the dogmatic differentiation of the West made by the papal institution as it developed in history.

To the question prevalent in our writers' time: When were the Latins condemned as heretics by the Orthodox Church? Neophytos responds that "Councils have censured the Latin belief concerning God, it being a heretical dogma." Thus, for Neophytos, the synodal condemnation of the *filioque* was simultaneously a condemnation of the Latins themselves, so that no other specific condemnation of them is deemed necessary. Among these Councils he lists the following: the Eighth Ecumenical Council presided over by Photios (879); the Council at which Michael Cerularios presided (1054); the Council presided over by Gregory II of Constantinople (1283–1289), "which cut off the Latins from the plenum of the Orthodox and disinherited them from God's Church"; the Council of Sergius II of Constantinople (999–1019), who deleted the name of Sergius Pope of Rome from the diptychs of the Eastern Church; the Councils during the reigns of Emperors Alexios, John, and Manuel Comnenoi (11th–12th century); the Council of the three Patriarchs in the East after the Council of Florence (1482); and Local Councils in Russia, Moldovlachia, and elsewhere.¹⁷⁵

On the basis of the above ecclesiological presuppositions, the Latins, as heretics, "are not capable of administering baptism, for they lost the grace to administer sacraments,"

---

173 *O*, p. 445.

174 *O*, p. 485.

175 *E*, p. 147 vi. Cf. *O*, p. 450ff. See V. I. Pheidas, Θεολογικός διάλογος Ὀρθοδόξου καί Ῥωμαιοκαθολικῆς Ἐκκλησίας ἀπό τοῦ σχίσματος μέχρι τῆς Ἁλώσεως [*Theological and Dialogue of the Orthodox and Roman Catholic Churches from the Schism to the Fall*], (Athens, 1975).

as St. Nikodemos observes.[176] They have no baptism, according to Neophytos, for they lack "the sound confession of the Trinity."[177] Thus, their baptism "deviates from the faith," according to St. Basil,[178] since, "by introducing pagan polyarchy into the monarchic Trinity, the Latins are godless," and consequently "unbaptized."[179] However, they are also "unbaptized" in the literal sense, according to St. Nikodemos; for "they do not preserve the three immersions," and thus *do not have the Church's baptism*.[180] Neophytos observes that, "since they are nowise immersed, i.e. *baptized*," they are unbaptized.[181] A. Parios reiterates the same.[182]

Oikonomos further adds that just as the slightest alteration in the sacrament of the holy Eucharist is condemned by the Church, in that it revokes the very sacrament; so likewise in baptism, even the slightest alteration cannot be tolerated.[183] In the case of the Latins, though, innovation was not limited to the elimination of the immersions and emersions. But, in accordance with the secular, modernistic spirit prevalent in the West, it has gradually extended to other areas of the sacrament as well, so that their rite has departed even further from the Church's one baptism.[184]

---

176 *P*, p. 56. Cf. *P*, pp. 509, 605.

177 *E*, p. 139.

178 *E*, p. 145.

179 *E*, p. 142.

180 *P*, p. 55. This is the position of E. Argentis. See Ware, p. 93.

181 *E*, p. 127.

182 *M*, pp. 263f, 265f. The Latins "are altogether unbaptized and worse than the Eunomians. Even if the latter did not in fact baptize with three immersions…yet they did baptize with at least one."

183 *O*, p. 441 (n. 1).

184 *O*, pp. 445f, 457. Cf. E. Simantirakis, Ἡ παρὰ τοῖς Πωμαιοκαθολικοῖς τελεσιουργία τῶν μυστηρίων τοῦ Βαπτίσματος, τοῦ Σρίσματος καὶ τῆς Θ. Εὐχαριστίας [*The Roman Catholic Ceremony of the Sacraments of Baptism, Chrismation and the Holy Eucharist*], (Athens, 1979), p. 141.

Chapter III: Application of the Canon   73

Hence, the one fundamental innovation gave rise to all the rest. The departure from Orthodox-patristic spirituality also brought on the differences in the dogmas. The dogmatic differences, therefore, are not to be looked at scholastically, but patristically and spiritually.

2. Latins are "in need of baptism"

So, the question arises: Given that the Latins are now heretics, can the Second Ecumenical Council's provisional distinction concerning Arians and Macedonians also be applied to them; and thus "by *economia*" can they be received by chrismation alone without being baptized? As we saw above, in interpreting Canon VII of the Second Ecumenical Council, our writers understood that the Second Council accepted the baptisms of the aforesaid heretics because they preserved the form of the Apostolic baptism which the Church never abandoned, i.e. the three immersions, which is a "true baptism," a βάπτισμα (tr. dipping) in the literal sense. So, the question is whether, given this stipulation, the Latin "baptism" can be accepted as "Apostolic baptism."

The West maintained that their baptism in no way differed from the Apostolic baptism. Oikonomos, however, responds that "affusion" (i.e. pouring), and much less "aspersion" (i.e. sprinkling), cannot ever be considered baptism. The first is an "uncanonical innovation,"[185] while the second is "unscriptural"[186] and void of the character of the "proper and true baptism,"[187] according to the holy Fathers.[188] Of course, Oikonomos is not referring here to

---

185 *O*, p. 398.
186 *O*, p. 436.
187 *O*, p. 430.
188 Athanasios the Great, whether speaking literally or metaphorically, was the first to condemn heretical "aspersion." *Discourse II Against the Arians* 43, *PG*

cases of "emergency" baptism, which even he does not rule out. These, however, are performed within the Church, in contrast to those who receive the "baptism" of whichever heresy and who thus receive death instead of life. What he has in mind here is what is done "without urgent necessity,"[189] being a practice arbitrarily sanctioned in the West.[190] This practice began with Pope Stephen I (253–257),[191] and was dogmatized by the Council of Trent (1545–1563), in accordance with the spirit of the West to "canonize" and legalize every innovation. But in no way can this innovation be justified,[192] being as it is a practice "odious to God,"[193] for it destroys the sacrament's God-ordered oneness.[194]

Furthermore, according to St. Nikodemos, the Latin baptism is "falsely so-called."[195] Oikonomos, in many pages, analyzes the meaning of "to baptize," from a literary, patristic, and scriptural point of view, in order to show that no metaphorical use of the term is possible.[196] To those who insist, however, that the Orthodox and Latin baptisms are

---

26:237B: "…so that he who is sprinkled by them is defiled in impiety rather than redeemed." Oikonomos comments: "In making this declaration, did not the divine Father with such foresight manifestly anticipate and likewise condemn the Latin aspersion as being invalid?" *O*, p. 424. For the views of other Fathers, see *O*, p. 425f. Cf. *P*, p. 52ff.

189 *O*, p. 398. It is the fruit of the "papal arbitrariness." *O*, p. 449.

190 *O*, pp. 424, 450-451.

191 *O*, pp. 448f, 452.

192 *E*, p. 147 xx. It is contrary not only to the Church's tradition (Acts ch. 8; Canons VII of the Second Ecumenical Council and XIX of the First, etc.), but above all to "Christ's dual baptism, the one in the Jordan," and "the one by the cross," as well as to "the burial in the tomb, the figure of which is baptism by three immersions."

193 *O*, pp. 424, 485. According to Neophytos, affusion is "accursed," while aspersion is "defiled." *E*, p. 147 xviii.

194 *O*, p. 454.

195 *P*, pp. 55, 56.

196 *O*, pp. 401f, 406ff, where the arguments of the opposite view are found.

Chapter III: Application of the Canon

identical, Oikonomos poses this question: "If Latin baptism is equivalent to ours, then why is it necessary to anoint them with divine chrism when they join us, as if they had not been chrismated at all? For the Latins have chrismation too. But if this is unacceptable for us (as are all other sacraments performed by them), then why not also their baptism by aspersion?"[197]

Our writers repeatedly found it necessary to refute the disserting view asserted not only by the Latins, but also by "their unsalaried defenders"[198] (i.e. Latinizers within the Church), regarding the canonicity of their "baptism." We shall, of course, concentrate on the more significant. These are an example of pure scholastic sophistry, but they acquaint us with the intellectual climate of the time, and help us to see the splendid theological weaponry of our theologians from their responses.

Thus, the view had been stated that, since even the most minute particle of the consecrated bread "is the whole body of Christ," consequently, even "a drop" of sanctified water

---

197 *O*, p. 456. In a detailed analysis, Oikonomos states the differences between "one who is baptized" and "one who is sprinkled":
1) The former "is buried, as one dead, in a grave," and "again rises," in "imitation of the Lord." The latter, "when he is poured upon, stands erect," and "neither goes down nor comes up again…as from a grave";
2) The former, "with his own body, depicts the three-day burial and resurrection." The latter "does not himself depict the mystery at all" since he does not participate in the actual event. And by aspersion, he undergoes "a strange and unnatural…burial";
3) The former "has the grave…into which…he descends." The latter "carries the grave, as it were, hanging over his head, and from there going down to his feet. And what could be more counterfeit than this?" True, Oikonomos cannot escape the criticism that in making these distinctions he is being scholastic. Yet, what he is seeking to do is to make the following truth perfectly clear: "And simply speaking, the affusion bears no likeness whatsoever to Christ's death, nor is he who is poured upon planted together with Him." *O*, p. 482f (n.).

198 *P*, p. 56.

"has all the power of baptism." Neophytos' response is as follows: "The consecrated bread of the Eucharist, before communion, and in communion, and after communion, and simply even when no one communicates it, is nonetheless the body of Christ. Baptismal water, on the other hand, is and is called baptism not before the immersion, nor after the immersion, but only in the actual immersion, i.e. actual use; before and after, it is merely baptismal water, not baptism." Moreover, at baptism we do not have a "drink," but a "deluge"[199] (according to St. Dionysios Areopagite: "complete covering").[200]

In response to the argument that the Latin aspersion "contains sanctification and grace by virtue of the invocations of the Holy Trinity," St. Nikodemos says that "baptism is not consummated by the invocations of the Trinity alone, but also necessarily requires the image of the Lord's death and burial and resurrection." Belief in the Holy Trinity, even when correct, must be supplemented by the "belief in the Messiah's death."[201] The mere invocation of the Holy Trinity does not sanctify the procedural violation of the sacrament.[202] Thus, according to St. Nikodemos, "since… the Latins are not planted together with Christ the dual-natured Seed in the baptismal water, then neither is their body fashioned by God, nor their soul; and simply speaking, they cannot burgeon salvation, but they wither and perish."[203] Neophytos comments that the Lord "ordained birth by water and spirit. But it is not she who sprinkles who gives birth, but she who is pregnant. Likewise, it is not the

---

199 *E*, p. 147 xvi.
200 *On Ecclesiastical Hierarchies* 2, viii. *PG* 3:397B.
201 *P*, p. 65.
202 *O*, p. 438. Cf. *O*, p. 424.
203 *P*, p. 65.

sprinkled fetus that is born, but the one that was carried in the womb."[204] The conclusion drawn from the above is given by Oikonomos as follows: "So, the Latin aspersion, being destitute of the immersions and emersions, is consequently also destitute of the image of the Lord's three-day death and burial and resurrection...and destitute of all grace, and sanctification, and remission of sins."[205]

Justified, of course, was the question: Why cannot "the same likeness of death" also be expressed through affusion or aspersion? Oikonomos' answer centers around the following four points: 1) the Latin innovation is an "intentional" violation of the Lord's commandment and the Church's tradition; 2) it is contrary to the single and canonical Apostolic tradition; 3) it alters the meaning of "to baptize"; and 4) it is contrary "to the Apostolic likeness of the death, and the burial, and the resurrection of Christ, as this likeness was interpreted by all the divine Fathers."[206]

Our writers consider flimsy the argument that chrismation remedies the "deficiency" with respect to the procedure of the Latin baptism. It does not follow, says Neophytos, that through chrismation the Latin baptism becomes "acceptable," inasmuch as chrismation is distinct from baptism; it constitutes a separate sacrament, and makes the already baptized person a participant in Christ's kingdom (cf. Canon XLVIII of Laodicea). One, therefore, who has not been canonically baptized and regenerated cannot become "a participant in Christ by mere chrismation," since man's regeneration is not accomplished through chrismation, but

---

204 *E*, p. 147 xvi.
205 *O*, p. 482f.
206 *O*, p. 482 n.

through baptism, which "also unites him with the likeness of Christ's death" (cf. Rom. 6:5).[207]

Likewise very often stated was the argument of the so-called "clinical" baptism.[208] In fact, it was upon this argument that the Council presided over by the Archbishop of Athens Chrysostomos Papadopoulos in 1932 based its renowned decision.[209] According to Anastasios Christophilopoulos, clinical baptism was administered *by affusion*. Even so, the Church always viewed with skepticism those persons who received such a baptism,[210] and thus, if they recovered, they were deprived of the right to be ordained, for their baptism was considered imperfect.[211] Of course, to the above sophism one could simply respond that the clinical baptism, in whatever way administered, took place not in heresy, but within the Church! In any event, Neophytos' response to this argument is that this kind of baptism is contrary to the word of the Lord, who "did not also teach us to baptize by affusion."[212] Therefore, he adds, no matter how these people had been baptized, i.e. by affusion or by aspersion, if they survived, "they were no less [considered] in need of baptism."[213]

Oikonomos offers a different, and therefore interesting, explanation: "When *out of necessity* they baptized such bed-

---

207 *E*, p. 147xiii.

208 An earlier reference has been found in Cyprian, Epist. 76, 12–13. Ad Magnum. *PL* 3:1195/6.

209 See Theocletos Stragkas, Ἐκκλησίας Ἑλλάδος Ἱστορία ἐκ πηγῶν ἀψευδῶν [*History of the Church of Greece from Reliable Sources*], vol. IV (Athens, 1972), pp. 1844–1847. For a critique of this decision, see Kotsonis, *(Problems…)*, pp. 191–192.

210 *(Greek Ecclesiastical Law)*, p. 114 and n. 2.

211 See Canons XII of Neocaesarea, and XLVII of Laodicea. *O*, p. 415f.

212 *E*, p. 147 xvi.

213 *E*, pp. 147 xvi, 147 xix.

Chapter III: Application of the Canon

ridden persons...they did not merely sprinkle them (in the Latin fashion), nor did they pour the hallowed water over their head, but thoroughly drenched their entire body (in Latin: *perfundebant*)."[214] This kind of baptism would not be repeated, "but it was considered an imperfect seal."[215] So, according to him, clinical baptism cannot be admitted as an argument in favor of the Latin aspersion. For it was permitted "out of necessity, and partly," and therefore "does not make it a law of the Church."[216] The Latin aspersion, on the other hand, is done "intentionally and without necessity."[217] Furthermore—and this is most essential—the Latin baptism is not a "drenching" like clinical baptism, but a sprinkling, and it is administered by sprinkled priests devoid of priesthood and unbaptized.[218] But if we accept their aspersion, then we also have to accept the rest of their sacraments, which is impossible according to Apostolic Canon XLVI.[219]

Thus, our writers conclude that the Latin baptism "deviated both in practice and in faith."[220] Since it is administered in heresy, i.e. outside the Church, it is in itself without substance (Apostolic Canon XLVII). It cannot be accepted by *economia* when Latins convert,[221] for it is

---

214 *O*, p. 414f; Cf. St. Cyprian, Epist. 76, Ad Magnum.

215 *O*, p. 414.

216 *O*, p. 416.

217 *O*, p. 417.

218 *Ibid.*

219 *E*, p. 147 ix. Cf. *P*, p. 89f; *O*, p. 492: "If *economia* is also exercised towards them, then I suppose their ordination must also be accepted..." For, according to Neophytos, "together with the acceptability of the heretical baptism admittedly also comes he who baptized, as one who has been ordained." *E*, p. 147 xxii.

220 *E*, p. 145.

221 *P*, p. 55. "The Latins' baptism is falsely called baptism, and therefore neither according to the principle of *acrivia* nor according to that of *economia*

imperfect, and is denounced by Canon VII of the Second Ecumenical Council as an unjustifiable innovation as regards the ritual. By the same Council, it is rejected together with the "single-immersion" baptism of the Eunomians, i.e. as being "inefficacious and ineffectual."[222]

Moreover, by rejecting the Church's tradition through this innovation of theirs, the Latins are, according to the Seventh Ecumenical Council (act viii), "anathematized."[223] Truly of the gravest import are the following questions posed by Oikonomos: 1) If there is a demand for the Latin aspersion to be accepted by *economia*, then why do not the Latins exercise some "*economia*" themselves, "and again resume what from the beginning was delivered to them from the Fathers and the Apostles, and abandon their innovations?"[224] And he continues: 2) "If he who joins the Church in fact accepts all the dogmas and sacraments of the Orthodox faith wholeheartedly and genuinely, and anathematizes all his patrimonial erroneous beliefs, how then does he hold as correct the wrongdoing with regard to baptism (the foundation of the faith)?"[225] And, 3) "If indeed the Church accepts the candidate's written statement, in which he anathematizes all his patrimonial erroneous beliefs, how then can she herself accept the innovation with

---

    is it acceptable." Oikonomos, too, agrees: "How shall we receive them who were never baptized at all?" *O*, p. 489. Cf. A. Parios, *M*, p. 263. This is also the position of E. Argentis. See Ware, p. 90.

222 *O*, pp. 424, 449, 499. Cf. Neophytos, *E*, pp. 147 xiv, 147 xvii.

223 *E*, p. 147 xvii.

224 *O*, p. 457. St. Nikodemos also writes something similar. *P*, p. 304f.

225 *O*, p. 491. Cf. A. Parios, p. 264: "With what conscience does the Eastern [Orthodox] receive as though baptized him who by the authority of the Spirit is judged to be wholly unbaptized?"

Chapter III: Application of the Canon

regard to his baptism, it being one of the erroneous beliefs he anathematized?"[226]

One hundred years and more after Oikonomos posed them, these questions received the following reply by the Second Vatican Council: "The sacrament of baptism may be performed by immersion or by affusion. Baptism by immersion is the more indicated form, as it signifies the death and the resurrection of Christ. In accordance with our prevailing custom, *the sacrament of baptism will generally be performed by affusion*"!...[227]

In light of what has been said above, it is easy to understand why our writers maintain that the Latins cannot be placed in the category of the Arians and Macedonians for the *economia* of the Second Ecumenical Council to be also applicable to them. For, "they are not at all immersed, i.e. baptized, but sprinkled," according to Neophytos. If their aspersion counts as baptism, then "it is wholly necessary either to establish two baptisms, or having established the one, to reject that by trine immersion."[228] On this point also, Oikonomos comments that "the Latins...limp...on both legs as regards the correct baptismal rite; in the other words, as regards the three emersions and immersions, which the sons of Arius and Macedonius genuinely performed according to the Apostolic tradition."[229] Moreover, according to A. Parios, the Latins are in a worse position than the very Eunomians, who at least preserved one immersion.[230] As a consequence, according to Parios' epigrammatic expression, "they who

---

226 *O*, p. 455. Cf. A. Parios, *M*, p. 264.
227 See Simantirakis, p. 134.
228 *E*, p. 147 vii; cf. p. 131.
229 *O*, p. 445.
230 *M*, p. 265.

convert from the Latins must indisputably, indispensably, and necessarily be baptized."[231]

Of course, the baptizing of the Latins does not mean that the dogma, "I confess one baptism," is rejected. "No, not at all," replies Oikonomos regarding this.[232] "When the heretics are administered our rites," says Neophytos, "they are not being *re*baptized, but baptized."[233] For, as St. Nikodemos says, "their baptism belies its name."[234] Therefore, "the Canons baptize those who had received a different [baptism] contrary to church law, and thus overturn not the one and only true baptism, but every alien and pseudonymous human invention."[235] Consequently, the (re)baptizing of the Latins does not have the meaning of simply making them members of the Church, but above all of accomplishing in them the regeneration that sprinkling is incapable of imparting to them.

3. Explanation of the Orthodox Church's Action in Dealing with the Latins

In confronting the arguments of the Latins and Latinizers of their time, our theologians also found it necessary to explain the Orthodox Church's past action in dealing with the West. As we know, this action "was not single and uniform, but fluctuated between *acrivia* and *economia*," since

---

231 *M*, p. 263. Cf Neophytos, *E*, pp. 127, 143. *P*, pp. 589, 605.

232 *O*, p. 425; cf. p. 486. E. Argentis, too, affirms the same. See Ware, p. 97.

233 *E*, pp. 128, 143.

234 *P*, p. 58.

235 *O*, p. 426. The term "rebaptize" is often misused, observes Oikonomos; "that is, in respect to the heretics' own self-styled baptism, albeit spurious and false and not even baptism in the literal sense." Hence more correct is the term "baptize," "there being but one true baptism which we believe in, and which is never repeated a second time." *O*, p. 420 n. 1.

"this or that policy and action of the Church was usually determined by more general reasons and aims of greater benefit to her, or to avert any harm and danger threatening her."[236]

According to the *prevailing* view, after the schism the Orthodox Church recognized "the validity of the Latin sacraments,"[237] and indeed that of baptism. Upon their conversion, the Church applied Canon VII of the Second Ecumenical Council or XCV of Penthekte to them, or occasionally received them by a mere recantation of their foreign doctrines.[238] Even after the Crusades and the Council of Ferrara/Florence (1438–1439), when the relations between Orthodox and Latins became strained, and the stance of the Orthodox East in dealing with the Latins became more austere,[239] the East considered the application of Canon VII of the Second Ecumenical Council to be an adequate measure of defense, that is she received them by chrismation and a written statement. This action was officially ratified by the Local Council of Constantinople in 1484, with the participation, moreover, of all the Patriarchs of the East. This Council also wrote an appropriate service.[240] Thus, according to I. Karmiris (and also according to the arguments of the Latinizers and pro-westerners during the Turkish rule), the cases of "rebaptism" were exceptions, owing "to individual initiative," and "not to an authoritative decision of the Church."[241]

---

236 See Karmiris, vol. II, pp. 972–973. Cf. Ware, p. 66ff.
237 Karmiris, p. 979.
238 *Ibid.*
239 *Ibid.*, p. 980.
240 *Ibid.*, pp. 981–982, 987–989.
241 *Ibid.*, p. 979.

This custom, however, was overturned in 1755 under Cyril V, Patriarch of Constantinople, by the imposing of the (re)baptism of Latins and all Western converts in general,[242] again through the application of Canon VII of the Second Ecumenical Council and the other relevant Canons of the Church. This action, to this day the last "official" decision of the Orthodox Church,[243] was opposed by those who disagreed. It was considered to have subverted the decision of the Council of 1484. Because of its circumstantial character,[244] not having gained universal acceptance and application, it was often not adhered to. In addition, the practice of the Russian Church from 1667 differed from that of the other Orthodox Patriarchates, and indeed that of Constantinople.[245] This, then, is what is commonly accepted to this day concerning the issue in question.

Among our writers, Neophytos and C. Oikonomos deal with the history of the problem more extensively than the others. They begin by calling upon the testimony of those who reject the Latin "baptism."[246] Then they note the cases

---

242 Ibid., p. 984.

243 Androutsos, (Symbology...), p. 321. Papadopoulos, p. 447. Christophilopoulos, article in Θεολογία, pp. 203–204; cf. pp. 120–121. Gritsopoulos, Θ.Η.Ε. 7 (1965), col. 1196.

244 See, in this regard, Skouvaras, p. 52ff. Cf. Metropolitan Germanos, p. 309ff.

245 According to Kotsonis (Problems..., pp. 189–190), "as far as the Patriarchate of Constantinople is concerned...until 1756 [write 1755], it recognized 'by acrivia' the validity of the baptism of those coming over from the Western Church, whereas through the Oros of 1756 [write 1755], it rejected it." On the other hand, in the Russian Church, "until 1441, what prevailed as acrivia was that those coming over from the Western Church were to be baptized anew. But from 1666/7 and to this day, the Russian Church 'by acrivia' recognizes the validity of their baptism."

246 In this list Oikonomos includes, among others, Photios the Great (pp. 421f, 450f—he condemned the "single-immersion" baptism), Michael Cerularius (p. 460), Th. Valsamon (p. 463), Germanos II Patr. of Const. (p. 465), St. Meletios the Confessor (p. 466), Matthew Vlastaris (p. 467), St.

in which Latins were received by baptism, and likewise justify the cases (propounded by those who disagreed with them) wherein either the Latin "baptism" was overlooked as unimportant, or wherein the *economia* of the Second Ecumenical Council was exercised towards the Latins.[247] Their teaching specifically can be summarized as follows.

a) Until the Council of Florence

1) The Ecumenical Patriarch Michael Cerularius, in his epistle to Peter of Antioch, includes, together with the other Latin innovations, also their baptism "by one immersion."[248] According to Oikonomos, if this was not "declared to be a common crime of the entire Western Church," and thus specific measures were not taken, it is due to the fact that this type of baptism was not yet universally prevalent in the West, but "usually the Apostolic baptism" was administered.[249] It is significant, however, that the papal legate Humbert criticized the East for baptizing Latins.[250]

Mark of Ephesus (p. 470), Manuel the Rhetor (p. 474), Patriarch Jeremias II (475), Dositheos Patriarch of Jerusalem (p. 476), and Patriarch Jeremias III (p. 476).

247 On this point, Sergios Makraios is presented as a witness by Cyril's opponents. In his History, he declares that "...from the time of the schism until the year of our Lord 1750, that is both before and after the fall of Constantinople, they used to anoint converts with chrism according to the Definition enacted under Patriarch Symeon. Before [1750], the Eastern Church did not accuse the Western Church of rejecting the baptism instituted by the Lord and His Apostles, neither at that Council in Florence, nor afterwards." In, «Ὑπομνήματα ἐκκλησιαστικῆς ἱστορίας» ["Records of Church History"] by C. Sathas, *Μεσαιωνικὴ Βιβλιοθήκη*, vol. III (Venice, 1872), p. 403. We shall return below, however; for Makraios' text here was abridged! (See n. 314 below.)

248 Karmiris, vol. I, p. 342.

249 *O*, pp. 460–461.

250 *O*, p. 498. Cf. *E*, p. 147 ix.

2) Likewise, the Lateran Council of 1215 "accused the Greeks...that they baptize the Latins who join their Church." Since, however, according to Oikonomos, "the baptism by single immersion, or by affusion or aspersion, was sometimes performed by the West in some areas and only sporadically,...the Greeks baptized only those who had been baptized in this manner." And that is what the testimony of this Council is referring to.[251]

3) Even the "highly renowned exegete of the sacred Canons, Theodore Valsamon," affirms that "those baptized with one immersion are all to be baptized again," having in mind the practice of his time (12th–13th century).[252] True, a problem arises from his fifteenth reply, in which, explicitly referring to the Latins, he says: "Those of Latin descent should not be sanctified by the divine and immaculate mysteries [i.e. the Eucharist] at the hands of the priests,[253] unless they first declare their decision to desist from the Latin dogmas and customs, and are, in accordance with the Canons, catechized and made equal to the Orthodox." The problem, according to Oikonomos, lies in the fact that he did not expressly add, "and baptized." The answer, according to him, is that the Latins had not yet universally accepted the "baptism by one immersion." Therefore, so that the one group not be confused with the other, "he used more general terms, saying, 'in accordance with the Canons,' and the 'equality' of the converts with the Orthodox." "In saying Canons," he means XCV of the Sixth Council and VII of the Second.[254] And if Valsamon's contemporaries, the pro-union Nikitas Mytilineos Archbishop of Thessaloniki,

---

251 *O*, pp. 462–463. *P*, p. 56. *E*, p. 147 vii.

252 *O*, pp. 463, 498–499.

253 "Orthodox, that is," clarifies Oikonomos (p. 464).

254 *O*, pp. 463–464.

Chapter III: Application of the Canon 87

John of Kitros, and Demetrios Chomatinos Archbishop of Bulgaria, "say nothing about the baptism," this was so because the Franks, already masters of Constantinople, "were raging against the Orthodox"; but also they had in mind the three immersions which the Latins as yet still officially preserved.[255]

4) During the reign of the pro-union emperor John Dukas (1206), according to an "unverifiable" opinion, "it was synodically voted only to anoint with chrism those who join the Church." This, according to Oikonomos, is not curious, for "it was because of the current circumstances that such a decision was taken by a Local Council," given that the "genuine baptism" still survived in the West.[256] The uncertainty that prevailed in the East regarding the form of the Western baptism made the Orthodox hesitant to make a definite decision, this uncertainty, among other things, is apparent in the following words of Matthew Vlastares (in 1335): "If in fact, as some say, they baptize by one immersion…" The distance, therefore, but also the rupture in ecclesiastical communion, did not allow the Orthodox to have direct knowledge and to determine a specific position for dealing with the West.[257]

5) Someone anonymous,[258] writing against the Latins during the reign of Manuel Paleologos (1391-1396), and basing himself on Canon VII of the Second Ecumenical Council, remarks: "[The Canon] does not deem necessary the rebaptism of those who, equally as with us, were administered divine baptism by three immersions." Oikonomos points out here: "The prevailing order in

---

255 *O*, p. 464.

256 *O*, p. 466.

257 *O*, p. 467.

258 This would be Makarios of Ancyra. See *O*, p. 468 n. 1 (the note is by the editor Soph. Oikonomos).

the Orthodox Church, in accordance to be sure with the canonical definition, considered that the Latins were at that time still being administered the salvific baptism equally as with us." Besides, this work, he says, was written during a period of preparation for union talks,[259] and thus it avoided all acuteness in expression.

6) One of the strongest arguments of those of the opposite mind, however, was that nothing was said about the Latin baptism at the Council of Florence (1439). If the Latin innovation constituted such a significant difference, why was it not included in the list of topics for discussion? Oikonomos responds that the Council limited itself to the "five" most fundamental dogmatic differences; that is, "the already legislated papal illegalities,"[260] inasmuch as the innovation regarding baptism still had not yet become general practice in the West, nor been officially and synodally ratified, but continued to be *an occasional, local custom*.[261] Neophytos adds that other differences too were not discussed at Florence, such as fasting on Saturdays, kneeling on Sundays, divorce of the clergy, eating of blood and strangled animals, etc., for other reasons, but also "because of the hurry to return."[262] But, again according to Neophytos, even if this Council had decided something regarding this problem, its decision would not be of any special significance, for "correct sacramental practice, like Orthodoxy itself, has its origin and institution and proof not from what was said or done in Florence, but from the Evangelists and the Apostolic and synodal Canons." What is significant in this regard is primarily the practice of the early Church, rather than the

---

259 *O*, pp. 467–468, 502f.

260 *O*, pp. 469, 499.

261 "The evil was occasional and local. The Western Church had not yet adopted this or made it law by proclamation." *O*, p. 469.

262 *E*, p. 147 viii.

Chapter III: Application of the Canon

current tradition, and indeed of those who participated in the Council of Florence. "For is it because we lack proofs dating back any earlier than Florence that we must pay attention to—I am loathe to say traitors of the faith—men of but yesterday?"[263]

Of those who participated in this Council, St. Mark of Ephesus of course is of especial importance. He is usually presented as an unshakable argument in favor of receiving Latins by *economia*. For, while absolutely Orthodox as regards the faith, yet in testifying "about the Orthodox Church's universal practice," he admits that we chrismate those who come over to us from them (i.e. the Latins)…as being heretics";[264] that is, he affirms the way of *economia*. To this our writers respond as follows:

St. Mark and those around him, according to Neophytos, gave priority "to the faith issues." They did not deal with the problem of baptism, for "the baptism issue was secondary." It is, however, significant that St. Mark does bluntly call the Latins "heretics," and he does reject and "dauntlessly expose" the aspersion that was spreading among them, writing that "twofold are the baptisms" of the Greco-Latin Uniates.[265] St. Mark explicitly includes the Latins, as heretics, in the group of early heretics mentioned in Canon VII of the Second Ecumenical Council. If he seems to affirm their reception by chrismation, i.e. in the manner prescribed for the Arians and Macedonians, this, according to Oikonomos, is due to the fact that up until the Council of Trent (16th century)—and even up until the eighteenth century—"the Apostolic form" of baptism also survived in the West.

---

263 *E*, p. 147 vii.

264 Karmiris, vol. II, p. 981.

265 *E*, pp. 146, 147 viii. *O*, pp. 468, 499f. Cf. Karmiris, vol. I, p. 422: "two baptisms, one performed by trine immersion, and the other by pouring water over the head…"

Thus, St. Mark went along with the reception of Latins by *economia*, 1) to avoid repetition of the one baptism due to indiscriminate zeal or ignorance; and 2) as a concession, in order to expedite the union. Thus, St. Mark applies Canon VII of the Second Ecumenical Council to the Latins in part, receiving them "as having kept the form of the Apostolic baptism."[266]

b) After Florence

1) Concerning the Council of Constantinople in 1450, called "the last in *Hagia Sophia*,"[267] the argument was propounded that "this one also did not mention baptism,"[268] in spite of the fact that it dealt with the Latin innovations which led to the schism. Indeed, here we have a very strong argument, and even Oikonomos is forced to admit that this is "most extraordinary." His attempted critical analysis of the text leads to the conclusion that there is a "deletion of words" in the copying of the Acts of the Council.[269] Neophytos, however, in his own peculiar manner, responds to the problem with the following counterargument: "Well, then, I suppose we should not even chrismate Latins, since the aforesaid Council did not mention chrism, i.e. chrismation. And not only that, but I suppose we should also ordain for money, since it somehow attempts to applaud this as well!" He continues, though, with the observation

---

266 *O*, pp. 503, 504.

267 For the Acts of this questionable Council, see Dositheos, *Τόμος Καταλλαγῆς* (Jassy, 1692), p. 457ff. Cf. Archim. V. C. Stephanidis, *Ἐκκλησιαστικὴ Ἱστορία*, 2nd ed. (Athens, 1959), pp. 395-396.

268 *E*, p. 147 viii.

269 In the Acts we find the phrase: "Nor is the chrism immediately applied to the head of the baptized," without, however, there being any previous mention of baptism. "How could the innovation on baptism have been passed over in silence, it being such and so?" asks Oikonomos (p. 471).

that, before this Council, St. Mark had already expressed his view concerning the Latin innovation in baptism and had disapproved of it, and that this constituted the "opinion on the Latin baptism" of those synodal Fathers as well.[270]

2) Nevertheless, the Council of Constantinople in 1484 creates the greatest difficulties for an acceptance of our theologian's position on Latin baptism. This Council decided "only to anoint with chrism the Latins who come over to Orthodoxy,...after they submit a written statement of faith." In other words, it ranks them in the class of the Arians and Macedonians of the Second Ecumenical Council (Canon VII).[271] Both the *Kollyvades* and Oikonomos, of course, are well aware of this, but they offer the following response.

According to Oikonomos, "since among the Orthodox there existed no formula concerning the reception of these (i.e. the Latins) by concession (inasmuch as from the beginning most preserved...the *acrivia* of the Ecumenical Councils), this Council ruled to imitate the followers of St. Mark,"[272] and thus it took the above decision, again, inasmuch as in the West neither affusion nor aspersion had yet been synodally canonized.[273] Yet how can we explain the fact that this synodal decision was not universally accepted in the East, if it was an official decision of the Orthodox Church? For, even after this Council, "neither did the Latin baptism seem acceptable...nor did [the Orthodox] think of the Latins as having priesthood, referring to the innovation

---

270 *E*, p. 147 viii.
271 Karmiris, vol. II, pp. 981f, 987f. *O*, p. 473f. The decision of this Council, with some exceptions to be sure, was in force until 1755. Ware, p. 67.
272 *O*, p. 505.
273 Oikonomos sagaciously observes (pp. 473–4, n. 2), that in the Service published by the Council, baptism is not even listed among the differences, because the innovation had not yet become official.

regarding the rite which again had spread in many places."²⁷⁴ Hence, despite the synodally given solution and the composition of a special service, "the East, aiming with conviction at the *acrivia* of the holy Ecumenical Councils," in practice received Western converts by baptism, for they saw no benefit arising from the concession made by *economia*, but rather "harm...to the simpler and afflicted Orthodox."²⁷⁵

Moreover, it was observed that the cunning of the Latins had increased. For in their proselytization, they took advantage of the willingness on the part of the Orthodox to make this concession, and interpreted it as proving that there really was no difference between Orthodox and Latin baptism. From that time, continues Oikonomos, this custom [of baptizing converts] prevailed in the Great Church [i.e. the Ecumenical Patriarchate] and also in all the Patriarchates of the East to this day," the synodal decision notwithstanding.²⁷⁶

Neophytos and the rest offer a more realistic interpretation on this issue. The reason for the lack of daring on the part of our people to call the Latins heretics after the fall of Constantinople and to condemn their "baptism" was, according to them, the fear arising from the situation that had developed in the East. They avoided this "from cowardice alone," says Neophytos. And he cites the following testimony of George Scholarios: "For it is not ours, being in such a state of poverty and weakness, to use such epithets on a Church of such power..." This was the first

---

274 *O*, p. 474. Oikonomos relies on an anti-Latin work by Manuel the Rhetor of the Great Church (1550).

275 *O*, pp. 505–506.

276 *O*, p. 506. And he adds: "Also all our most ancient monasteries, such as those of Athos, etc., uphold this same conviction."

Chapter III: Application of the Canon

reason. However, Neophytos does not exclude the "hope of rectification" of the Latins, i.e. their conversion.[277]

St. Nikodemos responds in much the same way. In receiving the Latins by chrismation in accordance with the decision of 1484, the Church expressly declares that she considers them heretics.[278] The early Canons were, therefore, not annulled, but "the Church wanted to use some big *economia* on the Latins, having that great and holy Second Ecumenical Council as an example to this end."[279] That is to say that the saint discerns in the fourth and fifteenth centuries a similarity of conditions and decisions. Thus, he continues, whereas in earlier times the East baptized the Latins, "later they used the chrism method," i.e. the way of *economia*, "for it was not good, given the utter weakness of our nation, to further excite the fury of the Papacy." Besides, "much agitation" had been created among the Latins because of the pan-Orthodox rejection of the Council of Florence.[280] And while the Orthodox East groaned under the yoke of slavery, "the Papacy was at its height, and had all the power of the kings of Europe in its hands, whereas our kingdom was breathing its last. Hence, if this *economia* had not been exercised, it was imminent that the Pope would have roused the Latin nations against the East."[281] In other words, both before the fall of the Ruling City (i.e. Constantinople), but more so after, the political situation demanded avoiding by all means the irritation of the West which was hostile

---

277 *E*, p. 146. Cf. also what was said by Sylvester Syropoulos: "We are people enslaved to the Latins, and what we say will find no acceptance." *Vera Historia*, ch. 6:11. In V. Laurent, *Les "Mémoires" de Sylvestre Syropoulos sur le Concile de Florence* (Paris, 1971), pp. 534–536.

278 *P*, p. 56.

279 *Ibid.*

280 *P*, p. 57.

281 *P*, p. 56.

towards Orthodoxy. So, it was political and not ecclesiastical criteria that took precedence. Therefore he concludes: "With *economia* passed, the Apostolic Canons should resume their place."[282] This means that in his time (18th century) the West was incapable of politically threatening the nation under Turkish rule, and thus there was no reason to fear the West.

Athanasios Parios also offers a similar response: "Those who propound the so-called synodal decree of 1484, which received Latin converts by chrismation, do not understand that the churchmen of that time were using *economia*, and that they thus formulated their decree because of the Papacy's agitation and tyranny." He, too, observes: "Now the season of *economia* has passed...and the papal fury no longer has any power over us."[283]

3) As it spread more and more, the innovation of the Latin baptism provoked reactions on the part of the Orthodox. This is apparent from the decision of a twenty-four bishop Council in the year 1600 in Constantinople, which decreed the reception of Latins by chrismation. This synodal formulation permits us, according to Oikonomos, to conclude that the East was in fact baptizing Latins. The decision of this Council can be explained "in two ways: for either it had in view the previously published earlier Definition (1484), without meddling with it any further," for as long as trine immersion survived in the West, the fear existed of repeating the correct baptism a second time;

---

282 *P*, p. 57.

283 *M*, pp. 267–268. Of course, the opposite opinion has also been stated. E.g. Ware writes in this connection: "Neither of these Councils [i.e. Constantinople, 1484, and Moscow, 1667] was exposed to foreign pressure or acted from fear of Papist reprisals; why then did they reach conclusions so different from those of Argenti?" (p. 95). Is this certain? And even if there were no immediate dangers, was the prevailing situation, at least in the Balkans, of no consequence? See below Oikonomos' explanation of this case also.

Chapter III: Application of the Canon 95

or, for the sake of *economia*, "to mollify the West's…brutal impulses and attacks," and to attract them to Orthodoxy.[284]

4) The Council of Moscow in 1620–21 decided to baptize Western converts.[285,286] However, the "great" Council of Moscow in 1666–67, in which the Patriarchs of Alexandria and Antioch also participated, approved the decision of the 1484 Council of Constantinople, and thus rejected the (re)baptism of Western converts.

The decision of this Council is explained by Oikonomos as follows: a) the Council of Moscow wished to remain loyal to the Council of Constantinople; b) Czar Alexios "was forced by local circumstances" to side in favor of such a decision, because of the inroads of the "neighboring pro-Latin Poles and Lithuanians, and especially those among them who had become Uniates"; c) this Council in no way conflicted with that of 1621, for the first "voted in accordance with *acrivia*," while this one "in accordance with concession." But "concession" was possible for the following reason. Among Russia's "enemies" were Uniates who had received "the genuine baptism of the Church." Hence, the Council "correctly combined *acrivia* with concession," so that the baptism of the Uniates who became Orthodox not be repeated a second time, and so as to attract the Latins more easily, after the example of Mark of Ephesus; d) this

---

[284] *O*, pp. 474–475.

[285] *O*, pp. 476, 507.

[286] Ed. In Russia, Latins and other heretics were received by baptism prior to the 1620 Council. At this Council, Patriarch Philaret (Romanov) of Moscow stated, "Since the beginning of the state of Moscow until now, there has never been a case where Latin heretics and heretics of other faiths were not baptized, except for the case of Ignatius the Patriarch, who was deposed from his episcopal throne." Patriarch Ignatius of Moscow had been deposed in 1606 for receiving a Latin convert by chrismation rather than baptism. See An Orthodox Ethos Publication, *On the Reception of the Heterodox into the Orthodox Church: The Patristic Consensus and Criteria*, (Florence, AZ: Uncut Mountain Press, 2023), pp. 219–230.

concession was confined within Russia and was not practiced in the other Patriarchates, just as the decision of 1484 had also not taken a universal character.[287],[288]

5) The Patriarch of Jerusalem Dositheos, although he accepts the "concessive discernment" of Mark of Ephesus, is nevertheless in favor of baptizing the Latins, in accordance with *acrivia*.[289]

6) The reply in 1718 of Ecumenical Patriarch Jeremias III to Czar Peter the Great, i.e. to receive Latins "by mere chrismation," had in view only the situation in Russia, and the "internal peace of…that multi-ethnic realm of Orthodoxy."[290]

7) Finally, the Council of Constantinople at which Cyril V presided in 1755 decided and imposed the baptism of Latins,[291] the decision of 1484 notwithstanding. The

---

[287] *O*, pp. 507–509.

[288] Ed. Another factors that led to the 1666–1667 Moscow decision to no longer accept Latins by baptism as had been practiced up to that point, was the influence of Latin Scholastic teaching on theology in Russia and in territories under Ottoman rule. At this council, the decision to stop receiving Latins by baptism was promoted particularly by Patriarch Macarius III of Antioch who had pledged his allegiance to the Pope of Rome prior to this council and was essentially a secret Uniate. This council has been controversial, particularly for the anathemas issued against the "Old Rite," liturgical rites that had been used in Russia prior to the reforms of Patriarch Nikon, and the severe persecution that was then endorsed against those who refused to accept the New or Nikonian Rite. In 1974, the Moscow Patriarchate declared the anathemas of this council to be null and void but the Latin Scholastic teachings concerning the reception of the heterodox have nevertheless continued to be perpetuated within and outside of Russia. See An Orthodox Ethos Publication, *On the Reception of the Heterodox into the Orthodox Church: The Patristic Consensus and Criteria*, (Florence, AZ: Uncut Mountain Press, 2023), pp. 233–276.

[289] *O*, p. 509. "For they who (without necessary cause) are not baptized with three emersions and immersions are in danger of being unbaptized. Wherefore the Latins, who perform baptism by aspersion, commit mortal sin." *Dodekavivlos*, p. 525; in *O*, p. 509.

[290] *O*, pp. 509–510.

[291] *O*, pp. 477ff, 510ff. The *"Oros"* of this Council (July 1755) was generally

Chapter III: Application of the Canon   97

Council's Definition (known as the *Oros*), which was also signed by the Patriarchs of Alexandria and Jerusalem, continues to be the Orthodox Church's last official decision on the issue.[292] Regarding its application during the eighteenth century, Neophytos notes: "Let me also point out, for the sake of the coming generation," that, as regards the Latins, while Mark of Ephesus baptized "with reserve," and "the bishop of Smyrna baptized openly," Cyril V, on the other hand, ordered "all to be baptized." And after Cyril, the Ecumenical Patriarch Sophronios II (1774–1780), "in the Great Church publicly also baptizes the Armenians, the Arians, and the Nestorians together with the Latins who join the Church, and by his own example has predisposed his people everywhere to do the same."[293] It is also known that the Ecumenical Patriarch Procopios (1785–1789) enforced the *Oros* even on the Uniates who converted in 1786.[294]

---

dated 1756, for that is when it was first published in print in the work, Ραντισμοῦ Στηλίτευσις [*A Denunciation of Sprinkling*], (pp. clxxiii–clxxvi). (Reprinted in Mansi 38:617-622. See also Appendix II below.) The work, *A Denunciation of Sprinkling*, was formerly considered to have been written by E. Argentis (e.g. see *O*, pp. 477, 511), but it is rather the work of Christophoros Aitolos. See Ware, p. 99.

292 S. Runciman, *The Great Church in Captivity* (Oxford, 1968), p. 359. Runciman calls the *Oros* "a result of a sincere conviction."

293 *E*, p. 147 xxv.

294 Karmiris, vol. II, p. 984 n. 4.

CHAPTER IV
Critical Evaluation

1. The Position of the Ecumenical Patriarchate

FROM THE preceding historical review based on the testimony of our writers, we come away with a picture quite different from the one we had until now. For example, according to I. Karmiris, "the *few* [sic] instances of rebaptism of Latins can be explained by the rousing of passions during the time of the Crusades, and by the doubts *of certain Orthodox* [sic] concerning the canonicity and validity of the Latin baptism by aspersion, which had by then become general practice in the West."[295] But according to our writers, the (re)baptism of Western converts was essentially the rule.[296] It was the political

---

295 *Ibid*, p. 981 n.

296 Ed. "The earliest norm in Russia for the reception of Western Christians, first Roman Catholics and later Protestants, into the Orthodox Church was by (re)baptism. In doing this, the Russian Church was in line with the Church of Constantinople." Fr. George Dragas, quoted in An Orthodox Ethos Publication, *On the Reception of the Heterodox into the Orthodox Church: The Patristic Consensus and Criteria*, (Florence, AZ: Uncut Mountain Press, 2023),

Chapter IV: Critical Evaluation

threat from the West that led to the application of *economia* and not *acrivia*. But this incidental use of *economia* had as necessary dogmatic-canonical condition the continued existence in the liturgical practice of the West, even until the eighteenth century, of the canonical baptism also; in other words, the fear of doing it again a second time. Of course, in both of these two views we can discern a 'tendency' of sorts. The first aims at justifying the way of *economia*, while the second the way of *acrivia*. We are assisted in finding the truth better still through a combination of the two.

In connection with this, however, the question unavoidably arises of how well our theologians' explanation is historically substantiated. Their basic position is that the (re)baptism of Latins was not imposed originally, for, in addition to the innovation, the canonical form of baptism was also prevalent in the West until the Council of Trent; hence the fear of repeating it a second time.[297] To be sure, the problem became more serious in cases of Orthodox who had Latinized (Uniates), and indeed upon their return to Orthodoxy. But let us see how Steven Runciman, the renowned historian of the Turkish rule, explains the Orthodox position: "The problem often arose because of the number of Greeks born in Venetian territory, such

---

p. 225, also see pp. 201–209.

[297] Ed. See previous footnote. It is unclear what the statement is based on, that reception of Latins by *economia* was out of fear of repeating a baptism a second time. According to Apostolic Canons 46, 47, and 50, the only time a person cannot be baptized in the Orthodox Church is if they already were baptized in the Orthodox Church in three immersions in the name of the Holy Trinity. Since baptisms performed by heretics does not bestow the Holy Spirit and the remission of sins, there is no reason why they cannot be received into the Orthodox Church by baptism. Fr. George demonstrated that this was the understanding of the *Kollyvades* authors so it is unclear where these authors expressed that there was at any time in history a fear of baptizing Latins.

as the Ionian islands, who, either because they came to settle within the Ottoman Empire or because they married Orthodox spouses, wished to return to the Church of their forefathers."[298] Thus, the first to undertake to settle the issue was the Council of 1484, which exercised *economia*, despite the condemnation of the Latin innovation. In this way, the risk of repeating the canonical baptism a second time was definitely avoided. Yet, this decision was not universally accepted. For obviously the Western innovation regarding baptism was spreading daily. Runciman continues: "But as time went on doubts arose whether this [i.e. *economia*] was sufficient;... These doubts were not purely occasioned by dislike for the Latins, though that motive was certainly not absent, but from a genuine suspicion that the Latin ritual of baptism was not canonically correct."[299] This explains the gradual suppression of the decision of 1484 among the Orthodox, especially in the see of the Ecumenical Patriarchate, and also the "bold move" of Cyril V and his followers to proceed substantially and officially to abolish that decision through the official *Oros* of 1755, with the approval, moreover, of the Eastern Patriarchs. *And just the Oros of 1755 by itself proves that those who, after 1484, were "rebaptizing" the Latins were not "few."*

Besides, it can be verified historically that the position on this issue of certain Patriarchs and hierarchs in general, that is of the responsible ecclesiastical figures (and, in practice, official organs of administration), was usually more moderate than that of the theologians, the clergy and the people, and particularly the monks, during the Turkish rule.[300] Runciman provides us with sufficient information

---

298 Runciman, pp. 355–356.

299 *Ibid.*, p. 356.

300 *Ibid.*, pp. 356–357. The same thing is observed in the case of Cyril V. The best theologians of the time (e.g. E. Argentis, and E. Voulgaris), the

Chapter IV: Critical Evaluation

to form a clear picture on this point. In reference to the reply of Patriarch Jeremias II to Peter the Great (1718), which recommends to the latter not to (re)baptize Western converts, he comments: "But in saying so Jeremias did not speak for the whole of his Church. He had on his side the Phanariot aristocrats and intellectuals, who prided themselves on their Western culture and their freedom from bigotry, and most of the upper hierarchy, men many of whom owed their posts to Phanariot influence and many of whom came from the Ionian islands, where the Orthodox lived on good terms with the Catholics and conversion was frequent. Such men saw no need for changing the existing practice."[301] They obviously did not have the *inner presuppositions* that would have enabled them to evaluate these things in an Orthodox manner. And it is well known where the ever increasing intercourse between the Orthodox and Westerners was leading; namely, to the blunting of the Orthodox-patristic criteria.[302] And this, at times, was tolerated—and even encouraged—by the local bishops in Latin dominated areas. Hence, the axiom should not be ignored here either: Only the actions of the authentically Orthodox, that is of the saints who have seen God, constitute an expression of Orthodox self-understanding.[303]

---

populace, and the monks unreservedly sided with him.

301 *Ibid.*, pp. 356–357.

302 It is sufficient to study the work by P. Grigoriou, *Σχέσεις Καθολικῶν καί Ὀρθοδόξων* [*Catholic-Orthodox Relations*], (Athens, 1958). Thus, e.g. Joseph Doxas, Metropolitan of Sevasteia and President of Paronaxia, by a written document of his entrusted (in 1671) the duties of *spiritual father(!)* and *itinerant preacher(!)* to Capuchin monks! (pp. 11–12). For more on this subject, see G. D. Metallinos, *Vikentios Damodos, Θεολογία Δογματική κατά συντομίαν ἤ τε Συνταγμάτιον Θεολογικόν* (Athens, 1980), p. 36ff.

303 Ed. Since 1755, Athonite saints and elders up to the present time have agreed with the *Kollyvades* Fathers that heretics must all be received by

2. The Action of Patriarch Cyril V

On this point, the case of Cyril V is even more characteristic. The mere fact alone, as we said, that this Patriarch dared to overturn the synodal decision of 1484 shows how little accepted it had been by the Orthodox conscience.[304] The argument is usually propounded that the Orthodox position regarding the Latins would harden during periods when the passions were roused due to the political danger from the West. It is peculiar, though, that Cyril proceeded with his decision at a time of no particular tension, and moreover prompted by a mass accession of Latins from nearby Galatas to Orthodoxy.[305] We consider it useful to dwell momentarily on this particular case.

Runciman gives very interesting descriptions of Cyril, his co-workers, and his opponents. The Patriarch is characterized as being "of good education, who had risen to the hierarchy on his merits." The other metropolitans also recognized his ability, but they did not sympathize with him, and they fabricated many false accusations against him.[306] According to the British historian, there were

---

baptism in the Orthodox Church by three immersions in the name of the Holy Trinity and that those who have been received by *economia* are still in need of baptism. See An Orthodox Ethos Publication, *On the Reception of the Heterodox into the Orthodox Church: The Patristic Consensus and Criteria*, (Florence, AZ: Uncut Mountain Press, 2023), pp. 359–371.

304 Ed. Of course, not only did the Ecumenical Patriarch sign the 1755 *Oros* but also the Patriarch of Jerusalem as well as the Patriarch of Alexandria.

305 See *O*, p. 477. Metropolitan Germanos, p. 310. Skouvaras, p. 52. For a detailed exposition of the matter, see the work by Philaretos Vapheidis, Ἐκκλησιαστικὴ Ἱστορία, vol. iii 2 (Alexandria, 1928), p. 146ff.

306 Runciman, p. 357. Extremely significant is the description of the Patriarch given by Sergios Makraios. According to him, Cyril "was…straightforward in opinion; simple in manner, even if to some he seemed intricate, diversely opposing as he did the many schemes of his enemies; fond of virtue; benevolent; lenient; fond of learning, devoted as he was to reading the

Chapter IV: Critical Evaluation

material and personal motives for the negative reactions to him: "He laid heavy taxes on the metropolitanates and richer bishoprics and relieved the burden on the poorer congregations...but it infuriated the metropolitans."[307] So, whereas the populace (the "rabble," according to some theologians),[308] the monks, and theologians of Argentis' and E. Voulgaris' caliber agreed with the (re)baptism of Western converts and supported Cyril, a strong reaction arose on the part of the metropolitans. But, as Runciman observes: "...somewhat to their embarrassment, they found that they had become the allies of the envoys of the Catholic powers,[309] who at once protested to the Porte

---

divine books. Having chosen for himself the more perfect life-style, he therefore kept longer vigils and more protracted fasts, and he was fond of longer church services. And all in all, he seemed brave, sharp in regard to what needed to be done, vehement in reference to what was decreed, immovable and fearless in the face of resistance. Hence, he was known as a fervent zealot of Orthodox dogmas, and he was talked about and exceptionally loved by the entire populace, charming and drawing to himself the souls of all by the splendor of his personal virtues, even if detractors variously contrived to cover the true zeal of the man, calling him cunning, even as the heretics defamed as a heretic him who was most Orthodox..." See *Ἐκκλησιαστική Ἱστορία* by C. Sathas, *Μεσαιωνική Βιβλιοθήκη* (Venice, 1872), pp. 206–207. In other words, the celebrated Patriarch had all the marks of the "traditional" churchman, who followed the hesychastic tradition of the *Kollyvades*.

307 Runciman, p. 358.
308 "...and published under the pressure of the rabble," notes Karmiris, vol. II, p. 984. The historian-philologist T.A. Gritsopoulos writes: "In the anti-papist struggle, the religious took part, not the frenzied rabble." See the article, «Κύριλλος Ε'» in *Θ.Η.Ε.* 7 (1965), col. 1195. The opponents of Cyril and of (re)baptism were the first who rushed to characterize the populace as rabble ("rabble and a mob of people..." writes the versifier of "*Planosparaktes*"). See Skouvaras, p. 95.
309 Ware (p. 77) calls Cyril a "victim of an alliance between Latins and Orthodox." And S. Makraios likewise observes (p. 221): "Thus the hierarchs and the gentry of the nation wavered, being tossed about by the force of winds from without!"

against this insult to the Catholic Faith."[310] As regards the Patriarch of Antioch, who did not sign the *Oros* of 1755, this same historian writes: "The Patriarch of Antioch would have done so, had he not been on an alms-seeking visit to Russia and had his throne not been snatched in his absence by a usurper."[311] As for Argentis, Runciman accepts that he was "a passionate theologian" who supported rebaptism on theological grounds, but that "he received no sympathy from the intellectual circles in which he moved."[312]

To be sure, the opinions on Cyril and his decision on "rebaptism" are very contradictory.[313] We shall not deal with this problem here. Yet in speaking about his motives, as well as those of his opponents, we shall cite the primary sources, that is the synodal and other documents contemporary with Cyril, which, as far as we know, have not yet been taken seriously by those who portray Cyril in a negative light. Likewise, it should be emphasized here that any attempt to compose a historical picture of the Patriarch and his work cannot be considered correct or proven, at least academically speaking, if it is based on the "censorious" texts of the time, which in many ways are irresponsible and historically dubious, and which essentially

---

310 Runciman, pp. 358–359. And even Skouvaras accepts that the reaction of the hierarchs occurred because "the matter was stirred by Cyril inopportunely and thoughtlessly, without foreseeing its unfavorable effects on the relations of the Orthodox with the Christian world of the West, from which they always hoped to receive help and national recovery" (p. 54).

311 Runciman, p. 358. Ware (p. 76) also accepts that the Patriarch of Antioch refused to sign, "not because he disagreed with the Definition as such, but because Cyril lacked the support of his Metropolitans."

312 Runciman, p. 357.

313 It is sufficient to look at the position on this issue of but two writers, non-theologians: on the one hand, that of E. Skouvaras, who was influenced by Cyril's opponents; and on the other, that of T. A. Gritsopoulos, *Θ.Η.Ε.* 7 (1965), col. 1193–1197, and *E.E.B.Σ.*, vol. 29 (1959), pp. 367–389.

Chapter IV: Critical Evaluation

are nothing but libel. Hence, the official documents of that time give us the following picture.

Having in mind the Council of Trent's official synodal sanctioning of aspersion in the West, Patriarch Cyril denounces the Latin baptism as being "polluted," in accordance with the spirit of the early Fathers of the Church as indicated in the first part of this study.[314] Both he and his followers were characterized by those who disagreed with this as being "Calvinists," "Calvinist-minded," and "Lutherocalvinists."[315] It was customary, anyway, for all anti-papists either to seek the support of the Protestants, or, even without so doing, to be considered pro-Protestant, or even simply Protestant.

From the writings of Cyril's opponents, however, it appears that what was of primary concern for them was to preserve the existing peace and quiet. Thus, the synod of metropolitans of the Ecumenical Throne, among other things, writes against Cyril: "And then, what, at this time, is the necessity, or the demand, or the benefit to our Orthodox nation, of the teaching on rebaptism? Or what nations have come over to us that required us to deliberate on this? Without need, why should there be such a racket and disturbance and scandal?"[316] Their fear, as stated afterwards, was that "destructive and disastrous" evils would follow, and also 'defamations and disgraces

---

[314] See above page 41. Cf. Mansi 38:607C. Just the fact that the question was raised concerning the (re)baptism of the "Latins of Galatas" proves that there was a problem of alteration of the sacrament in the West. The historian Sergios Makraios also affirms this: "...for a time it seemed to the priests in Galatas worthy of wonder and discussion, whether to anoint with chrism the Latins joining Christ's blameless Church, or to baptize them, as having wholly rejected the Lord's baptism and preferred the inventions of their own priests" (p. 203; cf. pp. 220, 408f.).

[315] Skouvaras, pp.161, 194–195, 197, et al.

[316] Mansi 38:601.

and derision against the Orthodox, and also hate and animosity and persecutions..." And if matters were not rectified, they would later result in "great danger and a disastrous end."[317] They speak about the disturbance "which overtook the Church," at a time when the Great Church was distressed "woefully by the very heavy burden of excessive debts passed down and accumulated," and therefore she had no greater need than of peace.[318] Thus, they advocate preserving the officially prevailing practice, i.e. reception by chrismation and written statement.[319] Their aim of preserving the prevailing calm is evident from what they write against a certain book by Christophoros Aitolos (*A Denunciation of Sprinkling*).

This "booklet," they write, "has in no small measure disturbed Christ's Church and all of us, wishing as it does to create factions...and to provoke public uprising and division within the Orthodox establishment...For this reason, colleague hierarchs heretofore present in this queen of cities *took counsel with the prominent noble gentry of this pious City*...and we deduced that from this venomous snake shall arise many *adversities disastrous for the Church and the nation*. For this booklet...*which is causing such a disturbance and no incidental harm*, appears to be castigating the Latins. But in so doing,

---

317 *Ibid.*, col. 602.

318 *Decretum Synodale*... from 28 April 1755, in Mansi 38:611A f. Skouvaras, judging the attacks against Cyril, also accepts that "the Latins and Uniates saw this as a 'disturbance of the smooth social relations,' and 'an insult launched against their faith.'" The ambassadors of the Western kings were troubled. "They correctly perceived that with this spreading and becoming established, their interests within the borders of the Ottoman empire are in many ways harmed. Hence they tried to counteract it, both openly and behind the scenes." They fought Cyril, "cleverly rousing against him the Ottomans in power," while on the other hand, they "threatened to proceed with economic reprisals and to take religious countermeasures against the numerous Greek diaspora" (p. 53).

319 Mansi 38:611A–613A.

Chapter IV: Critical Evaluation

it imperceptibly falls into an ignorant misinterpretation of the words of holy Scripture and of the holy Fathers, as well as into overt Lutherocalvinist blasphemies. Therefore, we have unanimously resolved that we ought...to regard this booklet as spontaneous disaster, abominable, odious, unlawful, uncanonical, blasphemous, and excluded and rejected from Christ's Church and from the reading of the pious Orthodox."[320]

The official documents do not indicate any particular souring of relations with the Latins, and therefore the Patriarch's action was seen as "a bolt from the blue." Hence his opponents' arguments are in proportion primarily seasonal-circumstantial, and less theological. What is predominant in them is the fear of provoking disturbances because of the affront to the West. The metropolitans saw no reason to harden the position towards the West. On the contrary, they judged it absolutely necessary to preserve the peace and quiet. Thus, in unanimity with the prominent gentry and leaders, they expressed their opposition to Cyril's "unjustifiable" action, and felt they were adequately served by the decision of the Council of 1484. They maintained that the Latins "have never been judged by any Council or by our holy Fathers as being unbaptized and in need of rebaptism,"[321] incorrectly, of course, as we saw above.

Hence the question arises: What were Cyril's motives? In fact, Cyril was not motivated by any preceding strain with the West, as indicated above (cf. pp. 80f, 95ff). The Patriarch simply represented another tradition, namely the one described above by the *Kollyvades* and C. Oikonomos. With the spontaneous request of the Latins

---

320 Mansi 38:615AB. Apparently this book by Christophoros Aitolos circulated in manuscript form before its publication in 1756.

321 Mansi 38:613CD.

of Galatas to convert to Orthodoxy as the sole motivation, he proceeded with his well-known decision primarily for theological reasons. Moreover, it was the Orthodox priests of Galatas who posed the question to Cyril, "whether to anoint with chrism the Latins joining Christ's blameless Church, or to baptize them, as having wholly rejected the Lord's baptism..."[322] *This confirms that there existed widespread doubt concerning the validity of the Latin "baptism,"* in spite of the above words of the metropolitans. Cyril *simply permitted* the priests "to baptize the joining...Latins as being unbaptized."[323] This event, first of all, clearly proves that *the decision of 1484 had never been universally accepted*, as our writers maintained above. And the involvement of Eustratios Argentis in this issue is the biggest proof that Cyril's action cannot be understood apart from the theological-dogmatic presuppositions, given that the opposing metropolitans were also "vehement anti-papists,"[324] who preferred, however, to maintain a moderate attitude for the sake of peace.

To be sure, the reasons were never absent that made the Latin danger felt and the strain on Latin-Orthodox relations ever dawning anew. The age of Patriarch Cyril V knew a Rome which endeavored to conquer Orthodoxy by roundabout ways and means. Very simply, she circulated the claim that there was unanimity among the two Churches as far as the doctrines were concerned, and thus she drew in the Orthodox more easily. But here again is proof that Cyril's theological presuppositions were Orthodox-patristic, in contrast with his bishop opponents. For the latter did not perceive, as he did, the necessity of

---

322 Skouvaras, p. 52.
323 *Ibid.*
324 *Ibid.*, p. 53.

guarding the Orthodox fold through a clear demonstration of the existing essential differences, among which was the one observed in sacred baptism.[325]

We believe that the above case studies adequately prove the realism of our theologians' line of thought. These theologians do not deny that opposing views always existed among the Orthodox in their positions regarding the West. However, they also accept—and this too is proven to be true—that there existed—again, always—a significant segment of Orthodox who considered the Latins heretics, their sacraments without substance, and their (re)baptism wholly natural.[326] The use of *economia* even by representatives of this segment was due to the fact that aspersion in the West was not universally predominant.[327]

---

325 Cf. Vapheidis, p. 59. That Cyril's aim was to guard the Orthodox flock from proselytism by revealing the difference in the baptism is also repeatedly noted by the historian of Cyril's time, Sergios Makraios, p. 214f. And specifically he writes that Cyril "spoke against their innovation from the throne, and he permitted those who wished to censure the Latins' new inventions against the correct faith, and their strange beliefs, to speak out and to write without fear, *correctly judging hollow friendship more harmful than overt enmity*. For what evil, small or great, did they not do, fabricating friendship and pretending Christianity?" (p. 217).

326 Runciman accepts something to the same effect (p. 357).

327 Here we must return to Sergios Makraios' exposition (see above n. 247). He continues: "...for they preserved the ancient and God-given baptism; but even if something of this sort did occur in some places, i.e. affusion or aspersion *which later became prevalent, it was not common or known to all*. Actually, it was reported that something of this sort was being practiced in some places; it was an occasional error, not a crime of the Church at large. But because during the eighteenth ecclesiastical century the ill-introduced aspersion overflowed and abounded in the West, and the God-given baptism was rather neglected, or was converted into affusions and aspersions, she [i.e. the Church through Cyril] pronounced those who were thus sprinkled unbaptized, as not having received the God-given baptism, and urged that such converts be baptized. But she had not as yet issued an inviolable definition on this, hoping for the conversion and correction of the West, and for the purging of their faulty and irreconcilable ritual...,
hence, it is necessary to baptize those who come over to the Orthodox Church, some as

But after the imposition of aspersion in the Roman Catholic world by the Council of Trent, then even the slightest doubt disappeared. To this segment belonged Patriarch Cyril V, and also our writers. It was that segment which, standing its ground even today, sees the differences between Roman Catholicism and Orthodoxy in their real dimensions, i.e. not as mere ritual and administrative differentiations, but as buoys indicating the deep alteration which the Christian truth has sustained in the regions of the papal West.

3. The Policy in Russia

C. Oikonomos, however, also found himself forced to explain the opposite stands on Western baptism taken by the Church of Russia and the Ecumenical Patriarchate in his time. His answer is that the Russian Church does not overlook the *acrivia* of the holy Canons, despite her decision of 1667. Although they use *economia* in Russia, "they do not declare implacable war on the Church's perfect baptism by dismissing those who seek it."[328,329] Moreover, the Russian

---

being unbaptized, and others as being questionable because of the confusion regarding the ritual. So it was from this time on [i.e. the 18th cen.] that the Eastern Church began to cry out against the Western Church, accusing the latter of having rejected the Lord's baptism...and accordingly she pronounced those who had undergone affusion or aspersion unbaptized, and permitted her priests to baptize converts..." (pp. 408–409). So, in explaining the reason for Patriarch Cyril's decision and motives, S. Makraios accepts that it was then that "for the first time" an official decision was taken concerning (re)baptism of Western converts. And this is true. What is significant here, however, is that he describes these things in exactly the same way as our writers do, and indeed C. Oikonomos, who was aware of Makraios' text. Makraios does not condemn Cyril's decision in any way, but as an historian he is interested in showing why the East was forced to take such a decision, and when this occurred.

328 *O*, p. 513; cf. p. 486f.

329 Ed. Whether or not this was the case at the time, it has unfortunately become increasingly common that converts seeking to be received by

Chapter IV: Critical Evaluation

catechizers of Western converts "first and foremost instruct those who join about this *acrivia* of the Apostolic baptism, then about the reception by concession."[330] So, a discrepancy between the Churches such as this does not destroy the oneness of Orthodoxy, since the other Patriarchates accept "those perfected in Russia by concession as legitimate children."[331]

Of course, in his personal correspondence, and indeed with individuals residing in Russia, Oikonomos could not point-blank condemn the practice prevalent there, for he not only had moral but also worldly ties with the Church in Russia,[332] though he does not cease to side with the decision of Patriarch Cyril V (1755). He does not neglect, however, to reprove it indirectly, writing: "I honor and respect the Russian Church as the undefiled bride of Christ and inseparable from her Bridegroom, and in addition as my own benefactress, by which the Lord has done and shall do many great and marvelous things, as she unerringly and verily follows the rule of piety. Hence, I do not doubt that it was in a spirit of discernment that she chose the older rule, in accordance with which she accepts the baptism of the other Churches [sic], merely chrismating those who join when they renounce their patrimonial beliefs with a written statement and confess those of the Orthodox faith."[333] Later, though, speaking

---

baptism are refused and told they must be received by *economia* instead. This is not only true in some Russian Orthodox churches but in other Orthodox churches as well, likely due to Orthodox involvement in the Ecumenical Movement which has led to further confusion regarding ecclesiology and the boundaries of the Church.

330 *Ibid.*
331 *O*, p. 514.
332 He was receiving a lifetime pension from Russia.
333 *O*, pp. 486–487.

"about the attitude of the Orthodox Churches outside Russia," and advocating the necessity of exercising *acrivia* on the Latins, he asks: "What are we to do about the aspersion?...how shall we receive them who were never baptized at all?"[334] And elsewhere, addressing the recipient A. Stourzas, he openly recommends to the "local servants and ministers of the Church" in Russia to do the opposite, that is to exercise *acrivia*![335,336]

---

334 *O*, p. 489.

335 *O*, p. 480f. Oikonomos maintained that if *economia* be deemed necessary by an "Ecumenical Council," "in any case, the Church of Christ shall do what is deemed right." And he continues: "The individual servants and ministers of the Church… speaking what befits sound doctrine…shall not act unjustly towards the most sacred rules of our Fathers on account of the reconciliation of those who had been separated, by spinning flax and wool together, and by accepting what is vainly propounded by the heterodox in defense and justification of the unlawful innovations which have been dared by them… And when they, who from heresies wish to come over to Orthodoxy, for one reason or another request the concession and *economia* regarding baptism, to them the approved and unashamed laborer of God shall unadulteratedly teach aright the word of truth when he catechizes them, gently instructing and reminding them that it is not arrogance which prescribes the divine laws and resolves the restitution by rejection."

336 Ed. It is notable that St. Paisius (Velichkovsky) (+1794), who was from Russia and studied theology in Kiev before departing for Mt. Athos, agreed with St. Nikodemos and the *Kollyvades* Fathers that all heretics, including the Latins, must be received by baptism, giving no heed to the decision of the Moscow Council of 1666–1667. We even see the two exchange letters for the support of baptizing those who never received the Orthodox Church's baptism (see Arhid. prof. dr. Ioan I. ICĂ jr*, "Despre Mirungere și Botez în Moldova anului 1785—starețul Paisie Velicikovski în dialog epistolar cu eruditul ieromonah Dorotheos Vulismas" (Sibiu, Romania: Revista Teologica, 2011), pp. 11–15). St. Paisius, through his disciples, revived the hesychastic and patristic tradition in Russia in the 19th century. St. Seraphim of Sarov, the Optina Elders, St. Theophan the Recluse, St. Ignatius (Brianchaninov) and countless other saints of that period were spiritual heirs of St. Paisius. See An Orthodox Ethos Publication, *On the Reception of the Heterodox into the Orthodox Church: The Patristic Consensus and Criteria*, (Florence, AZ: Uncut Mountain Press, 2023), pp. 306–313.

EPILOGUE

IN SUMMARIZING all that has been said above, we should emphasize that our writers begin with the specific ecclesiological and canonical presuppositions that we stated in the beginning. Remaining faithful to the principle set by Sts. Cyprian and Basil the Great, they side in favor of applying *acrivia* in receiving the various heretics; in other words, their (re)baptism. Of course, they do not deny the possible use of *economia*.[337] But, in the spirit of the Second (and Penthekte) Ecumenical Council, this is done "when it does not vitally harm" the Church, according to Oikonomos;[338] in other words, when the irrevocable stipulation set by these Ecumenical Councils is fulfilled: namely, that the sacrament of baptism has been administered in accordance with the Apostolic form. The use of *economia*, having a provisional and local character, does not do away with *acrivia* which constitutes the Church's canonical order. Therefore, "the

---

337 See *P*, pp. 53, 56–57. *O*, p. 511. And Neophytos (*E*, p. 147 xi), relying on Canon CII of Penthekte, also notes: "For it says we need to know both, the ways of *acrivia* and the ways of custom, and to follow the delivered form, i.e. the custom, and *acrivia* proportionately, not only for the penitent, but also, as has been shown, for those who convert from heresy."

338 *O*, p. 515.

one, holy, catholic and Apostolic Church of the Orthodox, having their salvation in view, both preserves the *acrivia* of the divine Canons, and also at various times and places apostolically resorts to *economia*, so as to receive those infirm in the faith, and to take care of incidental needs and difficulties, while avoiding incursions by the adversaries of Orthodoxy, until such time as she again restores *acrivia*."[339]

Our writers follow the same approach as those who were of the opposite mind and who classified the later heterodox (Latins) with those early heretics who, according to Canon VII of the Second Ecumenical Council, could be received without (re)baptism. They, too, apply the same Canon to the same heretics, only to arrive at the opposite conclusion, namely the rejection of *economia* in the case of the Latins. For in no way can their "aspersion" be considered baptism. And thus, faltering as regards the manner of the sacrament, they are classified under the proscriptive stipulation: "with only one immersion." Our writers defend this view canonically, historically, and dogmatically.

This position of theirs regarding the West cannot, in our judgement, be considered the product of prejudice or religious intolerance,[340] but the result of their purely Orthodox mind and their devotion to the faith and tradition of their Church. Aware of the West's penchant for innovations[341] and the alteration of the Church's tradition that was accomplished there with the passage of time, they fear that any and every concession could lead not only the

---

339 *O*, p. 511. Likewise, according to St. Nikodemos: "With *economia* passed, the Apostolic Canons should resume their place" *P*, p. 57.

340 Indicative of this are St. Nikodemos' remarks: "The erroneous beliefs and unlawful customs of the Latins and the other heretics we ought to abhor and shun. But if there be something in them that is correct and verified by the Canons of the holy Councils, this we ought not to abhor." *Eortodromion* (Venice, 1836), p. 584 n. Cf. Theocletos, Monk of Dionysiou, pp. 190–202, 287.

341 *O*, pp. 481, 484–485.

West, but the East as well, to even greater errors.[342] The application of *acrivia*, being canonically justified, guards Orthodoxy from slips of any kind.[343] Our writers appear to be absolutely convinced that in this way the issue is decisively resolved.

Nevertheless, diversity does exist in the Church's practice, and they cannot ignore this. To be sure, their intent is that the Church be led to exercise *acrivia* on the West. But this means that they, too, wished for a single manner of action, the attainment of agreement among the local Orthodox Churches, and the elimination of the noticeable irregularity. In other words, our writers as well as their opponents were in favor of a pan-Orthodox settlement of this problem. We also know that the necessity for a pan-Orthodox synodal decision has been judged urgent even after our writers.[344] In 1875, the Ecumenical Patriarchate expressed the wish "that the local Orthodox Churches might assemble together, [so that] the longed for official agreement on this issue might come to pass."[345] Since then,

---

342 "And if the reception of non-Orthodox by concession becomes generally formalized, then the genuine baptism will be in danger of being abandoned by the very Orthodox themselves (there being, unhappily, no one defending it)!" *O*, p. 514. There is evidence that, already in the United States of America, the Latin aspersion is also used by the Orthodox, and not canonical baptism! See Chrysostomos Stratman, *Orthodox Baptism and Economy* (Chicago, n.d.), p. 29.

343 "*Economia*, too, has its limits, and its measure of things, and its times, preserving the Church continually calm and unagitated and whole, lest by using too much *economia* she violate the law, and present her seasonal concessions and condescensions as being regular and of equal force with the *acrivia* of the divine laws from which she condescended" *O*, p. 433.

344 As early as Aug. 9, 1755, Ephraim Athenaios, later Patriarch of Jerusalem, in reaction to the Cyril V business, writes: "Since things are leading the Church to a great schism, a supreme high Council is necessary to order these matters in truth, with prayers and entreaties" (Mansi 38:631C; cf. 633B).

345 See Karmiris, vol. II, p. 978. The fact speaks for itself that from that time on, to the students of the Theological School of Halki were assigned scholarly

it has been repeatedly maintained by distinguished writers that a synodal settlement of the problem is necessary.[346]

From among our writers, Neophytos and Oikonomos deal with the idea of a pan-Orthodox settlement of the issue. The former touches upon the subject in passing, responding to the objection propounded at the time: "We should not abominate their (i.e. the Latins') aspersion prior to a Council." His reply is taken from the discourses of St. Athanasios on the Arians, and it is as follows: "...more capable than all men (and all Councils) is divine Scripture, and it requires those who believe in Christ not to be sprinkled, but baptized. 'And if a Council is needed concerning this,' says Athanasios, 'we have the works of the Fathers.' And indeed they were not remiss in this regard, but they wrote so adequately, that those who genuinely read their definitions are therefrom able to recall the truth proclaimed in the divine Scriptures. Therefore, concerning what is clear, there need be no Council assembled for what is sought."[347] So, according to Neophytos, no Council is necessary. Besides,

---

"theses" (and "dissertations") with the subject of the "baptism" of the non-Orthodox. Such are (in Greek): 1876, Nikephoros Zervos, "That the Orthodox and valid baptism is that which is performed by three immersions and the same number of emersions"; 1878, Anastasios Hatzipanayiotou, "Which is the valid baptism"; 1887, Amvrosios Galanakis, "That aspersion is an innovation"; 1913, Demetrios Karayiannidis, "The validity of heretical baptism"; 1917, George Garophalidis, "The validity of heretical baptism" (published); 1922, Gerasimos Kalokairinos, "What makes baptism valid"; 1937, Ioakeim Loukas, "The validity of heretical baptism"; 1947, Demetrios Demetriadis, "The place of the baptism of Catholics and Protestants who come over to Orthodoxy." (See V. Th. Stavridis, Ἡ Ἱερὰ Θεολογικὴ Σχολὴ τῆς Χάλκης [*The Sacred Theological School of Halki*], vol. I (1844–1923), Athens, 1970, and vol. II (1923 until today), Athens, 1968). A comparative study of these works would reveal the development of the Ecumenical Patriarchate's position and theology regarding non-Orthodox.

346 See Androutsos, *(Dogmatic...)*, p. 308. Same author, *(Symbology...)*, p.306. Karmiris, vol. II, p. 975.

347 *E*, p. 145. Cf. Athanasios the Great, *Letter on the Councils* 6, 1. *PG* 26:689AB.

it could not overturn the Church's already well-known decision anyway.

Discussion about a synodal resolution of the problem was repeatedly heard during the disputes of the eighteenth century when Cyril V was Patriarch. And in Oikonomos' time, this need was judged extremely urgent and was advocated chiefly by the supporters of *economia*. For, as far as the supporters of *acrivia* were concerned (our writers included), the Church had already resolved the issue. In this spirit, Oikonomos writes the following: "and even when, by divine summons and in Christ's name, for the union of the Churches, such an Ecumenical Council does convene, it shall lay down and delimit all those things that contribute to the bond of divine love and peace in the Holy Spirit (the arrogance of the innovation having disappeared like smoke)[348] ...and this Ecumenical Council shall order... nothing in any way contrary (perish the thought!) or opposed...to the Canons concerning the divine dogmas and sacraments and the ecclesiastical order as a whole, which have been laid down by the Apostles and by our holy Fathers, illumined by one and the same Spirit in the Councils whereby God spoke."[349] For it cannot "legislate that the aspersions and affusions can accomplish the same things as the one and only true baptism."[350]

This allows us to presume that if Roman Catholicism returns to the canonical manner of baptizing, then the use of *economia* would not be ruled out by Oikonomos (and, *cum grano salis*, even by the other *Kollyvades*). However, this ought to be decided on a pan-Orthodox level. This is what is meant by the following very significant words of Oikonomos: "If

---

348 An obvious allusion to Latin aspersion.
349 *O*, p. 480.
350 *Ibid.*

the Council deems it necessary for the Church in certain places (such as a large country comprised of many and diverse heretical ethnic groups), for the sake of evangelical *economia*, to consent for a short time to something that ought not to be (as Evlogios once said), and opportunely exercises a certain concession towards those who come over from heresies when any of them sincerely desire to enter life, but become less willing because of the *acrivia* of the Canon; in any case, the Church of Christ shall do what is deemed best, inasmuch as her Bridegroom remains with her inseparably until the end of time. He it is who preserves the *acrivia* of the divine dogmas and sacraments blameless and unadulterated in her, and Who enlightens her and guides her in the exercise of *economia*, in the proper place and time, towards those who join from without."[351] Of course, such an acceptance of Latin baptism by *economia* would in no way signify the validity of it "in itself," but only by virtue of the conversion of the Roman Catholic to Orthodoxy. Needless to say, the Papists' obdurate (as shown above) persistance in their innovations makes the exercise of any *economia* in the future questionable.

We believe that the following confession by C. Oikonomos ultimately articulates the spirit of the *Kollyvades* as well, and at the same time sums up their teaching: "We... praying night and day for the union of the Churches, accept and honor every *economia* as long as it does not harm our one mother the Church. We also have the salvation of her Orthodox sons in view, following in the footsteps of our blessed Fathers and teachers of the Church."[352]

The theological dispute described above might easily be characterized by many today as futile, or at least excessively

---

351 *O*, p. 480.
352 *O*, p. 515.

scholastic. Ultimately, it is nothing less than a fight to guard the continuity of the tradition, and to repulse the modernistic spirit of the West, using the particular means of a specific time.

What might be stated as a final conclusion based on the teaching of the Ecumenical Councils and the holy Fathers, which teaching our writers so lucidly and thoroughly present, is that for the conversion (i.e. entrance) to Orthodoxy of Latins and Western Christians in general, *economia* may be exercised only in such cases when a Christian Confession administered baptism with trine immersion and emersion according to its Apostolic and patristic form. When, on the other hand, this is not the case, but rather, despite knowing the truth, the innovation of aspersion or affusion was employed in a non-Orthodox manner (cf. relevant decision of Vatican II), then *acrivia* is judged mandatory.

Especially in our day when everything is considered relative, even in the ecclesiastical domain,[353] persistence in the tradition of the Saints is the most substantial counteraction against the general decline, even if such a position is ridiculed as lacking love. True love is the love for the truth in Christ.

---

353 Ed. On how reception by *economia* is often used to promote a heretical ecclesiology, see An Orthodox Ethos Publication, *On the Reception of the Heterodox into the Orthodox Church: The Patristic Consensus and Criteria*, (Florence, AZ: Uncut Mountain Press, 2023), pp. 373–384. "In 1971, the Russian Orthodox Church Outside of Russia issued a decree stating that, as a rule, all heretics should be received by baptism. This decision was based on a historical evaluation of the issue of the reception of converts in the Greek and Russian Churches as well as "the growth today of the heresy of ecumenism, which attempts to eradicate completely the distinction between Orthodoxy and all the heresies." Ibid., p. 382.

APPENDIX I

Holy Canons dealing with Baptism

1. Canons of the Holy Apostles (as recorded by Clement)

Canon XLVI (46)
We order that a bishop or presbyter that recognized the baptism or sacrifice of heretics be defrocked. For "what accord has Christ with Belial? Or what has a believer in common with an unbeliever?" (2 Cor. 6:15). (*P*, p. 51.)

Canon XLVII (47)
If a bishop or presbyter baptize anew anyone that has had a true baptism, or fail to baptize someone that had been polluted by the impious, let him be defrocked, on the grounds that he is mocking the cross and death of the Lord, and fails to distinguish priests from false priests. (*P*, p. 55.)

Canon L (50)
If a bishop or presbyter conduct an initiation [i.e. baptism] and perform not three immersions, but one

immersion—that administered into the Lord's death—let him be defrocked. For the Lord did not say, "Immerse [tr. Of Gk. verb βαπτίζειν] into my death"; but, "Go and make all the nations disciples, immersing them in the name of the Father, and of the Son, and of the Holy Spirit" (Mt. 28:19). (*P*, pp. 62–63.)

Canon LXVIII (68)

If a bishop, or presbyter, or deacon accept a second ordination from anyone, let him and he who ordained him be defrocked, unless it be established that he had been ordained by heretics. For those who are baptized or ordained by such cannot possibly be either believers or clerics. (*P*, p. 89.)

2. Canons of Ecumenical Councils

FIRST COUNCIL, 325 A.D.

Canon VIII (8)

Concerning those coming over to the catholic and Apostolic Church who at one time called themselves Catharoi, it seemed right to the holy and great Council that they have hands laid upon them and thus remain in the clergy. Above all, though, they should confess in writing that they will observe and follow the dogmas of the catholic and Apostolic Church. That is, that they will be in communion with persons married a second time, and with those who during the persecution lapsed from the faith (regarding whom a time has been fixed and a due season set [for penance]); so that they follow the dogmas of the catholic Church in everything. So, wherever—be it in small towns or in cities—any of them belonging to the clergy be the only ones ordained, they shall retain their clerical order. But if any come over where there is already a bishop of the catholic Church, lest there be two bishops in the city, the Church's bishop obviously shall hold the office of bishop, while the other, named bishop by the so-called Catharoi, shall have the honor of presbyter, except if it seem right to the bishop that he share the honor nominally. But if this be not to the bishop's liking, he shall devise for the other a position of either provincial bishop or presbyter, so that it appears that in every way he belongs to the clergy. (*P*, p. 133.)

Canon XIX (19)

Concerning those who belonged to the sect of the Paulianists, and who subsequently took refuge in the catholic Church, a definition has been promulgated that they be rebaptized without fail. If any of them, in the foregone interval, were examined as clergy, if they appeared to be blameless and irreproachable, after being rebaptized let them be ordained by the bishop of the catholic Church. But if the investigation finds them unsuitable, they ought to be defrocked. Likewise concerning the deaconesses, and in general concerning all those examined in the canonry, the same formula shall be closely observed. We made mention of the deaconesses who were examined as members of that order, for they have not even had the laying on of hands, so that without fail they are to be examined as laity. (*P*, p. 147.)

SECOND COUNCIL, 381 A.D.

Canon VII (7)

As for heretics who convert to Orthodoxy and join the portion of the saved, we receive them in accordance with the following procedure and custom: We receive Arians, and Macedonians, and Sabbatians, and Novatians who call themselves Catharoi and Aristeroi, and Tessareskaidekatitæ otherwise known as Tetraditæ, and Apollinarists, when they submit written statements, and anathematize every heresy that does not believe as the holy, catholic, and Apostolic Church of God believes, and are first sealed with holy Myron on the forehead, and the eyes, and the nose, and the mouth, and the ears; and in sealing them we say: "Seal of the gift of the Holy Spirit."

Eunomians, on the other hand, who are baptized with one immersion, and Montanists who in this [City] are called Phrygians, and Sabellians who teach the son-fatherhood [of Christ], and who do other evil things as well; and all other heresies (for there are many hereabout, especially those hailing from the region of the Galatians), all of them that wish to join Orthodoxy we receive as pagans. And on the first day we make them Christians; on the second, catechumens. Then on the third day we exorcise them with the threefold blowing into their face and ears. And then we catechize them, and oblige them to spend sufficient time in the church and to listen to the Scriptures. And then we baptize them. (*P*, p. 163.)

PENTHEKTE (I.E. SIXTH) COUNCIL, 691–692 A.D.

Canon XCV (95)

As for heretics who convert to Orthodoxy and join the portion of the saved, we receive them in accordance with the following procedure and custom: We receive Arians, and Macedonians, and Novatians who call themselves Catharoi and Aristeroi, and Tessareskaidekatitæ otherwise known as Tetraditæ, and Apollinarists, when they submit written statements, and anathematize every heresy that does not believe as the holy, catholic, and Apostolic Church of

God believes, and are first sealed, i.e. chrismated, with holy Myron on the forehead, and the eyes, and the nose, and the mouth, and the ears; and in sealing them we say: "Seal of the gift of the Holy Spirit."

Concerning the Paulianists, however, who subsequently took refuge in the catholic Church, a definition has been promulgated that they be rebaptized without fail. Eunomians who are baptized with one immersion, and Montanists who in this [City] are called Phrygians, and Sabellians who believe in the son-fatherhood [of Christ], and who do other evil things as well; and all other heresies (for there are many hereabout, especially those hailing from the region of the Galatians), all of them that wish to join Orthodoxy we receive as pagans. And on the first day we make them Christians; on the second, catechumens. Then on the third day we exorcise them with the threefold blowing into their face and ears. And then we catechize them, and oblige them to spend sufficient time in the church and to listen to the Scriptures. And then we baptize them. And likewise Manichaeans, and Valentinians, and Marcionites, and those from similar heresies.

Nestorians are required to make written statements, and to anathematize their heresy and Nestorios, Eutyches and Dioscoros and Severos, and the rest of the leaders of such heresies, as well as those who entertain their beliefs, and all the aforementioned heresies; and thus they may partake of Holy Communion. (*P*, p. 304.)

3. Local Councils

CARCHEDON-CARTHAGE, 258 A.D.

Canon [I] (of St. Cyprian)
While assembled in Council, beloved brethren, we read letters sent by you, concerning those among the heretics and schismatics presuming to be baptized who are coming over to the catholic Church which is one, in which we are baptized and regenerated. We are confident that by your doing these things concerning them, you yourselves hold fast to the stability of the catholic Church.

But since you are of the same communion with us, and so wished to inquire about this matter on account of our mutual love, we pronounce no recent opinion or one that has only now been established, but on the contrary we share with you and join you to that which of old was tested with all precision and care by our predecessors, and which by us has been observed. Decreeing now also by vote what we firmly and securely hold for all time, we declare that no one can possibly be baptized outside the catholic Church, there being but one baptism, and this existing only in the catholic Church. For it has been written: "They have forsaken me the fountain of living water, and they dug for themselves broken cisterns that cannot hold water" (Jer. 2:13). And, again, Holy Scripture forewarning says: "Keep away from another's water, and drink not from another's well" (cf. Pr. 5:15).

Also, the water must first be purified and sanctified by the priest, in order that it may be capable of washing away the sins of the person being baptized when he is thereinto immersed. And through the Prophet Ezekiel, the Lord says: "And I will sprinkle you with clean water, and cleanse you, and I will give you a new heart, and I will give you a new spirit" (Ezek. 36:25). But how can he who is himself unclean, and with whom there is no Holy Spirit, purify and sanctify water, with the Lord saying in the book of Numbers: "And everything the unclean man touches shall be unclean" (Num. 19:22)?

How can he who was not able to rid himself of his own sins, being as he is outside the Church, baptize and grant remission of sins to another? And even the question asked at the baptism is witness to the truth. For when we say to the examinee, "Do you believe you shall receive eternal life and remission of sins?" we are saying nothing else than that in the catholic Church remission of sins can be given, and that it is impossible to receive this from the heretics, where the Church is not. And that is why the advocates of the heretics are obliged either to ask the question, or to do justice to the truth, unless they attribute the Church to them also.

Moreover, it is necessary that he who has been baptized be chrismated, so that receiving the chrism he become a partaker of Christ. But the heretic cannot sanctify oil, seeing that he has neither altar nor Church. It is not possible for there to exist any chrism whatsoever among the heretics. For it is obvious to us that oil can by no means be sanctified among them for such worthy use. And we ought to know and not ignore that it has been written: "as for the oil of the sinner, let it not anoint my head," which the Holy Spirit even long ago declared in the Psalms (140:6); lest anyone be tracked down and led astray from the right way and be chrismated by the heretics, the enemies of Christ.

Furthermore, ho shall he who is not a priest, but sacrilegious and a sinner, pray for the one who was baptized, when the Bible says, "...God does not hear sinners; but if one is a worshipper of God and does His will, him He hears" (Jn. 9:31)?

We understand remission of sins as being given through the Church. But how can one give what he does not himself have? Or how can one do spiritual works when he himself has not received the Holy Spirit? For this reason he who comes over to the Church ought to be renewed, so that within [the Church] he be made holy by the holy, as it is written: "You shall be holy, even as I am Holy, says the Lord" (cf. Lev. 19:2; 20:7). And thus he who was deluded in error – being a man who, coming to God and seeking a priest, yet under the sway of error joined a sacrilegious [imposter] – might in the Church's true baptism put off this very error. For to accept with approval those whom the heretics [*Note in P*: some sources add *and schismatics*] have baptized is to endorse the baptism they administer. For one cannot be only partially capable. If he had the power to baptize, then he could also impart the Holy Spirit. But if he was incapable of giving the Holy Spirit, in that being outside [the Church] he does not have it to begin with, then he does not have the power to baptize anyone who might come to him.

Baptism being one, and the Holy Spirit being one, there is also but one Church, founded upon (Peter the Apostle of old confessing) oneness by Christ our Lord. And for this reason, whatever is performed by them [i.e. the heretics] is reprobate, being as it is counterfeit and void. For nothing can be acceptable or desirable to God which is performed by them, whom the Lord in the Gospels calls His foes and enemies: "Whoever is not with me is against me, and whoever does not gather with me scatters" (Mt. 12:30). And the blessed Apostle John, in keeping with the Lord's commands, wrote in his epistle: "You have heard that the Antichrist is coming, and now many antichrists have appeared" (1 Jn. 2:18). Hence we know it is the last hour. They came out from among us, but they were not from among us. Therefore, we too ought to understand and consider that the enemies of the Lord, and the so-called antichrists, would not be able to gratify the Lord. And therefore, we who have the Lord with us, and who hold fast to the unity of the Lord, abundantly supplied as we are in proportion to His excellence, and exercising His priesthood in the Church: we ought to disapprove, and refuse, and reject, and consider profane everything done by those opposed to Him, i.e. His foes the antichrists. And we ought to impart in full the mystery of divine power, unity, faith and truth unto those who from error and perversity come to us for knowledge of the Church's true faith. (*P*, pp. 368-369.)

COUNCIL OF LAODICEA, ca. 360 A.D.

Canon VII (7)

Concerning those who convert from the heresies of the Novatians, Photinians, or Tessareskaidecatitæ—be they their catechumens or their would-be believers—they are not to be admitted before they anathematize every heresy, and particularly the one in which they were bound; and thus their so-called believers, once they learn the beliefs of the faith and have been anointed with holy Chrism, may thenceforth partake of the holy Mysteries. (*P*, pp. 422-423.)

Canon VIII (8)

Concerning those who convert from the heresy of the so-called Phrygians, even if they be members of their imagined clergy, even if they be said to be of cardinal standing, they are to be catechized with all care and baptized by the Church's bishops and presbyters. (*P*, p. 423.)

Appendix I

COUNCIL OF CARTHAGE, 419 A.D.

Canon LVII (57)

[It is decreed] that rebaptisms, or reordinations, or transfers of bishops not be permitted to occur; and that he who wished not to conform to Your Holiness' gentle admonition and rectify his unpardonable [move] be forthwith prevented forcibly with the aid of the governmental authorities; and, when the established procedure has been carried out in connection with him, he not be judged [as though] a member of the Synod. (*P*, p. 491.)

Canon LXXX (80)

It so pleased [the Council] regarding the infants: Whenever reliable witnesses cannot be found who can say that without a doubt these have been baptized, nor be the infants themselves capable of answering in regards to any sacrament administered to them, on account of their very young age, these ought to be baptized without any hindrance, lest such a doubt deprive them of this extremely important purification by the sanctification. (*P*, p.503.)

4. The Canonical Letters of St. Basil the Great (d. 378 A.D.)

Canon I

The question of the Catharoi has been stated before, and you correctly recalled that it is necessary to follow the custom of those in each particular province, for they who at the time dealt with them were variously disposed towards their baptism. The [baptism] belonging to the Pepouzenoi, on the other hand, seems to me to be of no account, and I am surprised it escaped the great Dionysios, who himself wrote Canons. For the baptism which the early Fathers judged to accept is that which does not deviate from the faith in anything. Hence, some they called heresies, others schisms, and yet other conventicles. Heresies they called groups that had completely broken off and were estranged from the faith itself; schisms, groups that are at variance with one another for certain ecclesiastical reasons and over remediable issues; and conventicles, the gathering held by insubordinate presbyters or bishops and by the undisciplined laity. For example, when one of the clergy who was tried for an offense, and suspended from liturgizing, does not submit to the Canons, but claims the presidency and the liturgy for himself, and some people leave the catholic Church and follow after him, this is a conventicle. A schism, on the other hand, is to be at odds with those belonging to the Church over the issue of repentance [i.e. the readmission of the lapsed]. And heresies are groups such as the Manichaeans, Valentinians, and Marcionites, and these very Pepouzenoi; for the difference here concerns the very faith in God directly.

It therefore seemed best to those who dealt with this subject in the beginning to reject the [baptism] of the heretics completely, but to accept that of schismatics who were still considered to be of the Church.[354] Those people who were in conventicles, after improving themselves by proper repentance and by returning, were to be united once again to the Church, such being the case that the clergy who

---

354 Ed. Where St. Basil refers to schismatics as "ὡς ἔτι ἐκ τῆς Ἐκκλησίας ὄντων," this is more accurately translated "they formerly belonged to the Church." See An Orthodox Ethos Publication, *On the Reception of the Heterodox into the Orthodox Church: The Patristic Consensus and Criteria*, (Florence, AZ: Uncut Mountain Press, 2023), pp. 86–87.

had gone with the insubordinate were often received back into their former rank when they repented.

So, the Pepouzenoi are clearly heretics. For they blasphemed against the Holy Spirit by lawlessly and shamelessly assigning the name *Paraclete* to Montanos and Priscilla. On the one hand, then, they are condemned for deifying human beings; and on the other hand, they are doomed to eternal damnation because they insulted the Holy Spirit by comparing Him to human beings, and blasphemy against the Holy Spirit is unforgivable. What rationale, therefore, can there be for the approval of the baptism administered by those who baptize in Father, Son, and Montanos or Priscilla? They who were baptized in names not handed down to us were not really baptized. So, even if this escaped the great Dionysios, nevertheless we ought not to imitate the oversight. For the impropriety is self-evident and obvious to anyone who possesses even the slightest capacity for reason.

As for the Catharoi, they belong to the category of schismatics. Nevertheless it seemed best to the early Fathers (and I mean Cyprian, and our own Firmilian, and their circles) to treat them all—Catharoi, Encratitæ, Hydroparastatæ, and Apotactitæ—in one decision. For the beginning of the separation came about by schism, and those who revolted from the Church no longer possessed the grace of the Holy Spirit. For the imparting thereof ceased with the interruption of the continuity. True, the first ones to depart had had their ordinations from the Fathers, by the imposition of the hands of whom they possessed the spiritual gift. But in breaking away, they became laymen, and thus they had no authority either to baptize or to ordain, since they no longer had the power to grant others the grace of the Holy Spirit from which they themselves had fallen. Therefore [the early Fathers] ordered that such whom they regarded as having been baptized by laymen, when they come over to the Church, ought to be repurified by the Church's true baptism. But since it seemed best to some of the [bishops] in Asia to accept their baptism for the sake of the *economia* of the majority, let it be accepted.

Now we must pay special attention to the mischief of the Encratitæ. For, in order to make themselves unacceptable to the Church, they endeavored to anticipate through a peculiar baptism of their own; and in so doing they falsified their own custom. Therefore, I think that since there is nothing definitely prescribed regarding them, it behooves us to reject their baptism, and to baptize anyone coming over to the Church who had received it from them. If this is going to be an obstacle for the general exercise of *economia*, however, then we must again adopt the custom and follow the Fathers who regulated the ways of our Church with *economia*. For I fear lest, in wishing to make them hesitant about baptizing, we actually deter those who would be saved, because of the austerity of the measure. If they themselves keep our baptism [i.e. do not rebaptize converts from Orthodoxy], this should not urge us, for it is not our responsibility to return them a favor, but to serve the precision [Gk. *acrivia*] of the Canons. By all means let it be formulated that those who come over on the strength of that baptism of theirs be chrismated in full view of the faithful, and thereafter approach the Mysteries.

I am also aware that we have admitted to the seat of bishops the brothers in the party of Zoios and Satorninos who belonged to that class. Hence we can no longer distinguish from the Church those who were attached to their group, since by so accepting their bishops we have as it were made a Canon that establishes our communion with them. (*P*, pp. 586–588.)

Canon V (5)

We ought to admit those heretics who repent on their deathbed; admit them, that is, not indiscriminately, but examining whether the decision they exhibit for change of mind is genuine, and whether they have the fruits that witness to a zeal for salvation. (*P*, p. 592.)

Canon XX (20)

The women members of heresies who chose marriage after once vowing virginity, I do not think ought to be sentenced [when they convert to Orthodoxy]. "For whatever the law says it says to those who are under the law" (Rom. 3:19). Whereas they who have not yet come under they yoke of Christ do not yet know the Master's legislation either. Hence they are admissible into the Church, and together with all other sins they have forgiveness on this matter as well, as a consequence of their belief in Christ. And in general, what is committed in the catechumen state is not reckoned for liability, given that the Church does not receive these persons without baptism anyway. Such being the case, the privileges deriving from generation [i.e. the forgiveness of all former sins deriving from rebirth in baptism] are in this matter of utmost necessity. (*P*, p. 604.)

Canon XLVII (47)

Encratitæ and Saccophors and Apotactitæ all come under the same rule as the Novatians. For a Canon was promulgated concerning the latter, although it varies from place to place; whereas nothing specific has been said regarding the former. Be that as it may, we simply rebaptize such persons. If among yourselves this measure of rebaptizing is banned, as it most surely is among the Romans for the sake of some *economia* regarding their baptism, nevertheless let what we say prevail. For their heresy is something of an offshoot of the Marcionites who abominate marriage, and disdain wine, and say that God's creation is defiled. Therefore we do not receive them into the Church unless they be baptized in our baptism. And let them not say, "We have been baptized in the Father and the Son and the Holy Spirit," when they suppose—as they do in a manner rivaling Marcion and the rest of the heresies—that God is the maker of things evil. Hence if this please you, then more bishops must come together and thus set forth the Canon, so as to afford security to him who performs [rebaptism], and so that he who defends this practice might be considered trustworthy when responding on such matters. (*P*, p. 617.)

APPENDIX II

Oros of the Holy Great Church of Christ on the Baptism of Converts from the West (1755/56)

+ Many are the means by which we attain our salvation. And these, so to speak, in a ladderlike fashion are interlinked and interconnected, all aiming at one and the same end. First of all, then, is the baptism which God delivered to the sacred Apostles, such being the case that without it the rest are ineffectual. For it says: "Unless one is born of water and spirit, he cannot enter the kingdom of heaven."[355] The first manner of generation brought man into this mortal existence. It was therefore imperative, and necessarily so, that another, more mystical manner of generation be found, neither beginning in corruption nor terminating therein, whereby it would be possible for us to imitate the author of our salvation, Jesus Christ. For the baptismal water in the font takes the place of a womb, and there is birth for him who is born, as Chrysostom says;[356] while the Spirit which descends on the water has he the place of God who

---

355 John 3:5.
356 *PG* 59:153.

fashions the embryo. And just as He was placed in the tomb and on the third day returned to life, so likewise they who believe, going under the water instead of under the earth, in three immersions depict[357] in themselves the three-day grace of the Resurrection, the water being sanctified by the descent of the All-holy Spirit, so that the body might be illumined by the water which is visible, and the soul might receive sanctification by the Spirit which is invisible. For just as water in a cauldron partakes of the heat of the fire,[358] so the water in the front is likewise transmuted, by the action of the Spirit, into divine power. It cleanses those who are thus baptized and makes them worthy of adoption as sons. Not so, however, with those who are initiated in a different manner. Instead of cleansing and adoption, it renders them impure and sons of darkness.

Just three years ago, the question arose: When heretics come over to us, are their baptisms acceptable, given that these are administered contrary to the tradition of the holy Apostles and divine Fathers, and contrary to the custom and ordinance of the catholic and Apostolic Church? We, who by divine mercy were raised in the Orthodox Church, and who adhere to the canons of the sacred Apostles and divine Fathers, recognize only one Church, our holy, catholic, and Apostolic Church. It is her Mysteries [i.e. sacraments], and consequently her baptism, that we accept. On the other hand, we abhor, by common resolve, all rites not administered as the Holy Spirit commanded the sacred Apostles, and as the Church of Christ performs to this day. For they are the inventions of depraved men, and we regard them as strange and foreign to the whole Apostolic tradition. Therefore, we receive those who come over to us

---

357 Cf. Gregory of Nyssa, *PG* 46:585.
358 Cf. Cyril of Alexandria, *PG* 73:245.

from them as unholy and unbaptized. In this we follow our Lord Jesus Christ who commanded His disciples to baptize "in the name of the Father, and the Son, and the Holy Spirit";[359] we follow the sacred and divine Apostles who order us to baptize aspirants with three immersions and emersions, and in each immersion to say one name of the Holy Trinity;[360] we follow the sacred Dionysios, peer of the Apostles, who tells us "to dip the aspirant, stripped of every garment, three times in a font containing sanctified water and oil, having loudly proclaimed the threefold hypostasis of the divine Blessedness, and straightway to seal the newly baptized with the most divinely potent myron [i.e. chrism], and thereafter to make him a participant in the supersacramental Eucharist";[361] and we follow the Second[362] and Penthekte[363] holy Ecumenical Councils, which order us to receive as unbaptized those aspirants to Orthodoxy who were not baptized with three immersions and emersions, and in each immersion did not loudly invoke one of the divine hypostases, but were baptized in some other fashion.

We too, therefore, adhere to these divine and sacred decrees, and we reject and abhor baptisms belonging to heretics. For they disagree with and are alien to the divine Apostolic dictate. They are useless waters, as Sts. Ambrose and Athanasios the Great said. They give no sanctification to such as receive them, nor avail at all to the washing away of sins. We receive those who come over to the Orthodox faith, who were baptized without being baptized, as being unbaptized, and without danger we baptize them in

---

359 Matthew 28:19.
360 Apostolic Canon L (50).
361 *On Ecclesiastical Hierarchies* II, 7. *PG* 3:396.
362 Canon VII (7).
363 Canon XCV (95).

accordance with the Apostolic and synodal Canons, upon which Christ's holy and Apostolic and catholic Church, the common Mother of us all, firmly relies.

Together with this joint resolve and declaration of ours, we seal this our *Oros*, being as it is in agreement with the Apostolic and synodal dictates, and we certify it by our signatures.

In the year of salvation 1755,

+ Cyril, by God's mercy Archbishop of Constantinople New Rome, and Œcumenical Patriarch

+ Matthew, by God's mercy Pope and Patriarch of the great city of Alexandria, and Judge of the Œcumene

+ Parthenios, by God's mercy Patriarch of the holy city of Jerusalem and all Palestine

APPENDIX III

(Re)baptism of Latins on the Ionian Islands in the Nineteenth Century

THE *OROS* of the Eastern Patriarchs (1755), being the last official document on the problem of Western converts to Orthodoxy, was widely applied in the nineteenth century. The Orthodox bishops—those who were bearers and expounders of the tradition of Ecumenical Patriarch Cyril V and the *Kollyvades* Fathers—as a rule applied the *Oros*, and indeed in areas under foreign occupation, disdaining the consequences. Particularly where the fear was especially sensed that the dogmatic differences would be thought of as relative, due to the constant intercourse between the Orthodox and Latin populations, brave prelates did not hesitate to baptize Latin converts. Nor did they pay any heed to the dangers ensuing from their boldness.

One such area were the Ionian Islands, and particularly Kerkyra (Corfu), where until World War II the Roman Catholic element was always numerous and flourishing, and also politically very powerful. During our recent research at the Historical Archives of Kerkyra, we noted a series of cases, dating from 1824 onwards, of Roman Catholics converting to Orthodoxy through canonical baptism and not just by holy myron (i.e. chrismation). In these instances, this is requested by the Roman Catholic convert, and the Metropolitan (in this particular case, Makarios from Roga, 1824–1827)[364] grants the necessary permission.[365]

The proportions that the issue took appear from the secret correspondence of the English Commissioner of the Ionian Islands, Fred. Adam,[366] with his superior, the English Minister of Colonies, Lord Bathurst. We studied these letters at the Public Record Office of London, C(olonial) O(ffice) 136, in the summer of 1982. In one of these documents,[367] the English Minister informs Commissioner Adam that he had received complaints from the "Holy See" concerning a series of (re)baptisms of Latins in Kerkyra, and that the privileges given the "Papal Church" by the previous Commissioner John Maitland were thus being infringed upon.[368] Hence the Minister remarks to Adam: "Your attention is, therefore, directed to the attempt which it appears has recently been made to infuse into the minds of the people, the unwarrantable belief that baptism by a Roman Catholic Priest is not valid."[369] The Pope, moreover,

---

364 S. C. Papageorgiou, Ἱστορία τῆς Ἐκκλησίας τῆς Κερκύρας [*History of the Church of Kerkyra*], (Kerkyra, 1920), pp. 131–137.

365 Historical Archives of Kerkyra, Metropolitan's File no. 57, fol. 6–7.

366 On him, see Elias Tsitselis, Κεφαλληνιακὰ Σύμμικτα [*Cephalonian Miscellany*], vol. II (Athens, 1960), pp. 570–573.

367 P.R.O., C.O. 136/313. fol. 29–39, no. 104. Bathurst's document to F. Adam dated 14 Oct. 1826 (cf C.O. 136/188, fol. 296–304).

368 The English "Patronage" took upon itself to guarantee the vested interests of the Churches and religious minorities.

369 C.O. 136/313, fol. 36b. Bathurst's following comment is indicative of the prevailing climate: "As I observe, however, that it is at the same time admitted, that this second baptism is not performed publicly, but with the doors of the church closed, it is to be hoped that this has not by any means become a general practice, and that you will, therefore, have the less difficulty in suppressing it!" (fol. 36b–37a). It is true indeed that, under Western (Roman Catholic and Protestant) occupation, baptisms of Western

Appendix III

had charged that the Greek bishops were aspiring "to destroy the Catholic religion,"[370] and that the Greek bishop of Kerkyra in particular was proving to be "the most acrimonious enemy" of the Papal Church.[371] As a result, the Roman Catholics of Kerkyra were asking themselves if they were "Turks" or "Jews," since they were being (re)baptized! What is curious is that the Roman Catholics, familiar with the situation of "forced" smoothness of their relations with the Orthodox that prevailed until the end of Venetian rule (1797),[372] attributed Makarios' stance to…his different

> converts demanded great heroism; hence they were rare, or they were performed in secret and therefore remained unknown. A typical example is the case of the English Lord Frederick North-Guilford (1766–1827). In Jan. 1791, the English noble, the son of a Prime Minister, became Orthodox, by canonical baptism, according to his own demand. For, as he states in his own handwritten "Confession," he had not received this as an Anglican, and he believed Orthodoxy to be the "One, Holy, Catholic, and Apostolic Church," outside of which there are no sacraments. He took the name Demetrios. On this, see the study by Kallistos Ware (Bishop of Diokleia), "The Fifth Earl of Guilford (1766–1827) and his Secret Conversion to the Orthodox Church," *The Orthodox Churches and the West*, ed. D. Baker (*Studies in Church History*, vol. 13) (Oxford, 1976), pp. 247–256. Guilford is the most significant proof that baptisms of Western converts occurred even during the Venetian rule of the Ionian Islands, but they were kept secret for obvious reasons. And for years, Guilford, too, maintained absolute secrecy on this matter. See G. D. Metallinos, «Οἱ Τρεῖς Ἱεράρχαι 'Προστάται' τῆς Ἰονίου Ἀκαδημίας» ["The Three Hierarch 'Patrons' of the Ionian Academy"], *Ἀντίδωρον Πνευματικὸν* (volume in honor of G. I. Konidaris) (Athens, 1981), pp. 287–288; same author «Ἡ Ἰόνιος Ἀκαδημία—Κριτικὴ παρουσίαση τοῦ ὁμωνύμου βιβλίου τοῦ E. P. Henderson» ["The Ionian Academy – A critical presentation of E. P. Henderson's book by the same title"], *Παρνασσὸς* ΚΓ' (1981), p. 332ff.

370 Fol. 44f.

371 As stated in a Report by Roman Catholics of Kerkyra sent to the Vatican and communicated to London: "That schismatic bishop impudently boasts that 136 Catholics have gone over to the Greek religion since he held his high office" (1824), fol. 63b–64a.

372 See P. Grigoriou, *(Catholic-Orthodox Relations)* (Athens, 1958). From the Orthodox side, see Papageorgiou, p. 45ff, and particularly the special study by A. Ch. Tsitsas, *Ἡ Ἐκκλησία τῆς Κερκύρας κατὰ τὴν Λατινοκρατίαν 1267–1795*

education ("educated in Turkish Colleges...").[373] The outcome was that Adam stated in his relevant report that he assured the "Holy See" that the (re)baptism of Latins "should be prevented for the future"![374]

That the tradition represented by the *Kollyvades* Fathers and C. Oikonomos constituted the prevalent practice of the Church of Greece is apparent from the following study, published in 1869, when the Western spirit had begun to infiltrate the Orthodox East more intently and the first rays of a dawning Ecumenism could be discerned. The study is titled: "Epistolary Dissertation on Baptism, or Demonstration that when the Eastern Orthodox Church baptizes converts from other Churches, she is not rebaptizing but baptizing them, being as they are unbaptized," by D. Marinos, Prof. D. Th. (Hermoupolis, 1869, 70 pages). The island of Syros, and its capital Hermoupolis, was a center of the Protestant mission and also had a strong Catholic community, and the ever-memorable author refutes their claims.

For all that ecumenical relations obviously blunt fidelity to the Fathers, the Church of Greece—in principle at least—did not deviate from her standard practice. In

---

[*The Church of Kerkyra during the Latin Rule 1267–1795*], (Kerkyra, 1969). The prevailing conditions on the Ionian Islands and in the other areas under Latin rule are presupposed and depicted in the study by J. Kotsonis (ex-Archbishop of Athens), Ἡ ἀπὸ κανονικῆς ἀπόψεως ἀξία τῆς μυστηριακῆς ἐπικοινωνίας Ἀνατολικῶν καὶ Δυτικῶν ἐπί Φραγκοκρατίας καὶ Ἐνετοκρατίας [*The Merit of Sacramental Intercourse of Easterners and Westerners during the Frankish and Venetian Rules from a Canonical Point of View*], (Thessaloniki, 1957).

373 Fol. 66a. The criteria under which the Roman Catholics viewed the issue of the (re)baptisms are exhibited in the following questions which they submitted to the Vatican: "Is not this an affront to the Catholic and Roman Church? And what an insult to the Catholics residing in Corfu? *Ibid.* The spiritual, traditional and theological criteria were, already by that time, completely inert!

374 P.R.O., C.O. 136/38, fol. 13. Report by F. Adam to Bathurst from Kerkyra, 16 Jan. 1827.

Appendix III

order to facilitate ecumeni(sti)cal politics, however, in 1932 the Church of Greece under Archbishop Chrysostomos I (Papadopoulos)[375] disregarded the *Oros* of 1755, and introduced into the *Euchologion*[376] the "Service of Conversion to Orthodoxy from the Latin Church," thereby reinstating the practice of 1484, i.e. reception of Latins by *chrismation* and *written statement*. But even in this case, the Church of Greece—in accordance with her ecclesiology—never considered Western baptism valid "in itself," inasmuch as sanctifying and saving sacraments do not exist outside the Body of Christ, outside the one, true Church.

---

375 Karmiris, *The Dogmatic and Symbolic Monuments…*, vol. II, p. 991ff.

376 Μικρὸν Εὐχολόγιον ἢ Ἁγιασματάριον, 11th ed. (Athens: *Apostolike Diakonia* of the Church of Greece, 1992), pp. 110–113.

APPENDIX IV

Letter to the Œcumenical Patriarch Saint Gregory V

from

Saint Nicodemus the Hagiorite

(Late September–early October, 1806)
(Archives of Iveron Monastery)

Folio 1a:

> Most Holy, Most Divine, and Worshipful Lord
> And Master and Œcumenical Patriarch.

The bearer of this my letter, drawing his descent from Hungary and having been baptised, or to put it better, drowned and polluted by the Latins' pollution, through me doth approach your most holy Pate, fervently entreating that he might be baptised with the Orthodox Baptism of our own Eastern Church of Christ. Therefore, we implore, both he and I, your Christ-imitating and apostolic heart to send

Appendix IV

(by a two-liner injunction from you) the aforementioned unmonkish and uninitiated monk to the Wallachian Father Gregory the spiritual father, at the Monastery of the Pantocrator, so that that one, being of the same race and tongue, might initiate him and give him a new birth through our Baptism, so that both he and I may more earnestly entreat God that, along with all your other salvific desires, ye might also enjoy a favourable voyage and successfully return to your Œcumenical Throne[377] and act in imitation of the good, unto the common benefit of the entire Christian people.

    Imploring your prayers, I remain professing myself
your most lowly slave,
Nicodemus.

Folio 1b (By the hand of saint Gregory V the following note):

We pray.
Sir Nicodemus, in our behalf,
do what you have written.
+ Patriarch of Constantinople, Gregory

---

377 The holy Patriarch Gregory V, who was exiled on the Holy Mountain (at the monastery of Iveron), was recalled to the œcumenical throne on the 23rd of September 1806.

APPENDIX V

That Those Returning from the Latins Must Incontrovertibly, Indispensably, and Necessarily Be Baptized[378]

by

Saint Athanasius of Paros

The Catholic Church confesses one baptism for the remission of sins. The same holy Church also calls this "illumination," as we hear daily in the Liturgy of the Presanctified Gifts, "As many as are approaching illumination" and the rest. Now the same Catholic Church had received that this baptism, which is also called illumination and which bestows remission of sins, is to be performed with three immersions. For this reason, regarding those not baptized in three immersions, the holy and Œcumenical Second Council commands us to receive them like Greeks [i.e. pagans] and thus to baptize them.

---

378 First published by the hieromonk Theodoret Maurus in his book *Monasticism and Heresy*, Athens 1977, pp. 263–265.

Appendix V

So, let us consider. First of all, the Latin aspersion, inasmuch as it is administered by heretics, cannot be illumination. "For what communion hath light with darkness?" Therefore, neither can it be a baptism. Therefore, neither can it bestow remission of sins. Second, the baptism that is administered for the remission of sins is performed with three immersions. The Latin aspersion has not even a single immersion; therefore, not only is it not baptism, but it cannot even be called baptism. So, if the Latin aspersion is not illumination (as in truth it is not), and it cannot be called baptism (as it is indeed not called by those of right mind), then, I say, how can the Catholic Church receive him who returns from the Latin aspersion as one who has been baptized?

The seventh canon of the Second Œcumenical holy Council: "Those who from heresy turn to Orthodoxy, and the rest… But Eunomians, who are baptized with only one immersion, and the rest… we receive as heathen. On the first day we make them Christians; on the second, catechumens; on the third, we exorcise them by breathing thrice in their face and ears; and thus we instruct them and oblige them to spend some time in the Church, and to hear the Scriptures; and then we baptize them."

So, if this is to be done with those baptized in one immersion, the rest is obvious. Is not this canon a decision of the Holy Spirit? With what conscience, then, can the Easterner receive as one baptized him whom the Spirit's authority has classed as wholly unbaptized?

Moreover, does he not consider that he himself is going against even his own self? He commands the catechumen to anathematize all the innovations of Papism, and the latter anathematizes them completely. One of Papism's innovations is admittedly the subversion of the apostolic baptism, an innovation as great and dreadful as the danger of man's salvation. So, once that man has anathematized this innovation as well, that is to say aspersion, how and with what heart can the Easterner then confirm with the chrism the innovation that has just been anathematized? In truth, I am at a loss and shudder when I reflect on these things.

He who returns from a heresy anathematizes all innovation. Yet the Latin aspersion is itself also an innovation, as is also affusion.

So, the one returning from the Latins anathematizes the Latin aspersion and affusion as well.

If, however, the Latin-minded do not confess so, let them prove that aspersion is not a rejection of the three immersions—or that when a man anathematizes the innovations, he does not, along with the other innovations or rather even before the others (for the divine mystery of baptism is the beginning of Christianity), also anathematize aspersion, as having subverted the three immersions delivered by the divine Apostles, according to Basil the Great, the revealer of heavenly things. But if they cannot prove this to be the case, then let them listen.

That which is consigned to the anathema as an innovation can no longer be confirmed and sealed as sacred and holy.

Aspersion, however, is consigned to the anathema as an innovation by those returning from the Latins. Therefore, having been anathematized, aspersion can no longer be confirmed and sealed as sacred and holy. What could be clearer and more obvious than this?

St. Athanasius of Paros

UNCUT MOUNTAIN PRESS TITLES

Books by Archpriest Peter Heers

Fr. Peter Heers, *The Ecclesiological Renovation of Vatican II: An Orthodox Examination of Rome's Ecumenical Theology Regarding Baptism and the Church*, 2015

Fr. Peter Heers, *The Missionary Origins of Modern Ecumenism: Milestones Leading up to 1920*, 2007

Fr. Peter Heers, *Formation in the Love of Truth*, 2024

The Works of our Father Among the Saints, Nikodemos the Hagiorite

Vol. 1: *Exomologetarion: A Manual of Confession*

Vol. 2: *Concerning Frequent Communion of the Immaculate Mysteries of Christ*

Vol. 3: *Confession of Faith*

Other Available Titles

Elder Cleopa of Romania, *The Truth of our Faith*

Elder Cleopa of Romania, *The Truth of our Faith, Vol. II*

Fr. John Romanides, *Patristic Theology: The University Lectures of Fr. John Romanides*

Demetrios Aslanidis and Monk Damascene Grigoriatis, *Apostle to Zaire: The Life and Legacy of Blessed Father Cosmas of Grigoriou*

Protopresbyter Anastasios Gotsopoulos, *On Common Prayer with the Heterodox According to the Canons of the Church*

Robert Spencer, *The Church and the Pope*

G. M. Davis, *Antichrist: The Fulfillment of Globalization*

Athonite Fathers of the 20th Century, Vol. I

St. Gregory Palamas, *Apodictic Treatises on the Procession of the Holy Spirit*

St. Hilarion (Troitsky), *On the Dogma of the Church: An Historical Overview of the Sources of Ecclesiology*

Fr. Alexander Webster and Fr. Peter Heers, Editors, *Let No One Fear Death*

Subdeacon Nektarios Harrison, *Metropolitan Philaret of New York*

Elder George of Grigoriou, *Catholicism in the Light of Orthodoxy*

Archimandrite Ephraim Triandaphillopoulos, *Noetic Prayer as the Basis of Mission and the Struggle Against Heresy*

Dr. Nicholas Baldimtsis, *Life and Witness of St. Iakovos of Evia*

On the Reception of the Heterodox into the Orthodox Church: The Patristic Consensus and Criteria
Patrick (Craig) Truglia, *The Rise and Fall of the Papacy*
St. Raphael of Brooklyn, *In Defense of St. Cyprian*
The Divine Service of the Eighth Œcumenical Council
The Orthodox Patristic Witness Concerning Catholicism
Hieromartyr Seraphim (Zvezdinsky), *Homilies on the Divine Liturgy*
Abbe Guettée, *The Papacy*
St. Raphael of Brooklyn, *On the Steadfastness of the Orthodox Church*

Select Forthcoming Titles
Acts of the Eighth Ecumenical Council
Cell of the Resurrection, Mount Athos, *On the Mystery of Christ: An Athonite Catechism*
St. Hilarion (Troitsky), *Bible, Church, History: A Theological Examination*
Fr. Theodore Zisis, *Kollyvadica*
George (Pachymeres), *Errors of the Latins*
St. Maximus the Confessor, *Opuscula: Theological and Polemical Works*
Fr. Peter Heers, *Going Deeper in the Spiritual Life*
Fr. Peter Heers, *On the Body of Christ and Baptism*
Athonite Fathers of the 20th Century, Vol. II

This 2nd English Edition of
I CONFESS ONE BAPTISM...

written by Protopresbyter George D. Metallinos, D. Th., Ph. D. and edited by Uncut Mountain Press, typeset in Baskerville printed in this two thousand and twenty fourth year of our Lord's Holy Incarnation, is one of the many fine titles available from Uncut Mountain Press, translators and publishers of Orthodox Christian theological and spiritual literature. Find the book you are looking for at

uncutmountainpress.com

**GLORY BE TO GOD
FOR ALL THINGS**

AMEN.

www.ingramcontent.com/pod-product-compliance
Lightning Source LLC
Chambersburg PA
CBHW061748070526
44585CB00025B/2830